Ancient Cathedrals of Wales:
their story and music

ancient cathedrals of wales:

their story and music

Meurig Owen

ISBN: 978–1-84524-204-6

Cover design: Eirian Evans

First edition: 2013
Llygad Gwalch, 12 Iard yr Orsaf, Llanrwst,
Conwy, Wales LL26 0EH
☏: 01492 642031
✆: lona@carreg-gwalch.com
Website: www.carreg-gwalch.com

Also by Meurig Owen

Ways with Hazel and Horn (with Bob Gruff Jones)

A Grand Tour of North Wales

Gordon Wilyman – Memoirs of a Welsh Halfbred
(with Gordon Wilyman)

Brenhines y Bryniau

Hedges, Sticks and Baskets

Cofio'r Cefn – Cefn Remembered (ed)

William Parry Jones: Nant Meifod, Cresco, Tyn Rhyl

North Wales Male Voice Choirs

contents

prologue, acknowledgements and thanks

Little did I realise what I'd let myself in for. It had all started following the publication of my book on 'North Wales Male Voice Choirs' and the interesting question of what comes next! Writing about the choirs had been enjoyable, it had let me into a fascinating way of life; getting to know about the weekly rehearsal where hundreds of enthusiasts come together in a spirit of comradeship.

But I also realised that in this musical nation of ours there was yet more to be told, I had merely scratched the surface. What about music in our Cathedrals and its important part in church services for example? This was my proposal to publisher Myrddin ap Dafydd. He liked the idea but wanted more, he wanted a book on the ancient cathedrals which also encompassed the musical content!

That's how this book came to be written. Inevitably getting all this into one handy readable form was a challenge, almost a toe-in-the-water experience but quite a bit more than getting-a-flavour sort of book.

It meant a visit to all the Welsh Cathedrals, a particularly agreeable experience. From Bangor and St Asaph in the North, to St Davids, Llandaff and Newport in the South with Brecon roughly mid way. And in each place meeting so many people eager to tell me all they knew.

I must ask readers to forgive my indulgence over St Asaph where I have lived for twenty years and have known about all my life. As a child growing up in Cefn Meiriadog, for long closely linked with the city, remembering seeing Bishop Havard on his horse riding past the small farm where my family lived! Cefn parish was privileged, its first rector was Archdeacon D.R. Thomas who wrote the classic 'History of the Diocese of St Asaph' followed later by Canon John Fisher who with Baring Gould wrote the excellent 'Lives of the British Saints' (three volumes). Little wonder then that St Asaph, for good reason, may be just a wee bit over exposed in this book!

My thanks are due to several people and sources, cathedral guides, organists and musical directors, historians and cathedral staffs who have all been extremely helpful. Most are listed at the end of each chapter. Several books, and Cathedral Web pages, also listed, proved really worthwhile. And to Ceri Evans who kindly spotted and deleted the blemishes in the final draft! I must also thank The Archbishop of Wales, The Most Reverend Dr Barry Morgan for so readily agreeing to write the foreword.

Finally and above all to my wife Menna for all her love and help, ever ready to advise, proof-read at every stage and spur me on.

Meurig Owen
Spring 2012

Foreword by the Most Reverend Dr Barry Morgan, Archbishop of Wales

This book manages to say something about the history, architecture, important features and artefacts, as well as the music of the six Anglican cathedrals in Wales. That is quite a feat in a book of fewer than 200 pages. It has been, for Meurig Owen, a labour of love and the reader will be able to use it as a guide to the distinctive things each of the Welsh cathedrals has to offer, both to pilgrims and tourists. Welsh cathedrals are very modest in comparison with their English counterparts but all of them are built on ancient Christian sites. As the author reminds us, Christianity came to Wales long before Augustine came to Canterbury in 587 and the Welsh bishops, according to Bede, were none too impressed by him when they met at Aust on the South East border between England and Wales. It is also worth remembering, as this book does, that Bangor is probably the first territorial diocese in the British Isles as a result of King Maelgwn's invitation to Deiniol to have spiritual oversight of all his kingdom.

Here is a book with all the necessary detail for the visitor and a book which might encourage more people to visit these religious buildings '*made dirty with prayer*' over the centuries.

The Most Reverend Dr Barry Morgan
Archbishop of Wales and Bishop of Llandaff

part 1

acknowledging our debt to the celts, the romans and the gauls

How soon did Christianity come to Wales? Did the well travelled St Paul ever come here (to South Wales) on one of his missions as he journeyed westward? There are some who harbour that thought. If that event did occur, then Christianity would certainly have reached here before the end of the second century. During the Roman 500 year occupation of Britain too, Christianity was to gain credence, the coming and going of military personnel, some Christian converts, together with Emperor Constantine's conversion in 341 AD was to make sure of that. Writing in 'The Church Congress Exhibition Handbook, Newport, 1930' the Ven. Robert Williams, Archdeacon of Carmarthen reasoned that the source of our early Christianity 'according to all historical evidence points to Gaul as its country of origin', He then went on, 'Early in the third century, we are told , parts of the country not reached by the Romans were subject to Christ. Caerleon (Isca Silurum) gave the faith its two first native martyrs – Aaron and Julius – in the persecutions of Diocletan (304), and it is not impossible that there may have been a bishop in the "City of the Legions" in Roman times'.

When the Romans left in 410, ostensibly to protect their interests back in Italy, Britain was left to fend for itself. Saxons seeing a country weakened, then seized the opportunity to invade; much of the new found Christian influence came under siege. Put in simple terms, the Celts together with their new found faith and institutions were driven westward by the marauders. We're now in the 5th and 6th centuries popularly known as the 'Age of the Saints'.

The country is in a state of flux, the Celtic Saints sought refuge where they could, and we see them developing a monastic structure. Each town of consequence had a monastery/collegium with its self ruling Bishop or Abbot to evangelise the area.

By the time of St Augustine's second mission to Britain at the beginning of the 7th century to convert the Saxons as an envoy of Pope Gregory the Great, we see a fairly well ordered system in place among the British Bishops. They held to their own Easter date, based apparently on the Jewish Passover, their baptism, confirmation, and Holy Communion rites. Moreover they did not wish to be subordinated to the Pope and they certainly did not wish to evangelise among the Saxons who had massacred over a thousand monks at Bangor on Dee.

Also at issue was the Roman position of celibacy in the priesthood. The British custom allowed marriage of its bishops and for their sons to follow into the priesthood as of right. Augustine's mission looked for a joint effort to convert the Anglo Saxons to the Christian faith.

It is of interest here to note other facets of the British (Celtic) Church. Giraldus in the 12th century noticed particularly its characteristic care for the community.

Archdeacon D. R. Thomas refers interestingly to the Briton's insistence on cutting their hair – shaving the top of the head, and allowing a fringe around the sides to resemble our Lord's crown of thorns.

This then was the basis of the position they took at the Augustinian conference which was attended by seven British bishops. The Celtic Bishops decided to remain independent of Rome, holding fast to their own traditions and national identity. This was to continue until 768 when apparently the Cathedral Church at Bangor, during the episcopacy of Bishop Elfodd, accepted the Roman Catholic Order which opened the door to the Welsh Church eventually accepting the authority of Rome and furthermore we see a growing friendship with Canterbury. Indeed we see Archbishops of Canterbury consecrating bishops for Welsh Sees and sometimes exercising discipline over them. 'Wales had lost nothing by the fusion of the churches', says Archdeacon Williams, 'True unity can be realised in and through variety, and Wales gained much by participating in a larger life than would have been possible in a state of provincial isolation'.

In a discussion about the Celtic Saints it is worth noting that they probably came into the shell vacated by the pagan druids. Some even adopted their practice of cursing an enemy. Pagan shrines and wells were adopted for the purpose of worship. The wells became centres of pilgrimages as at Holywell in Flintshire. Miracle cures were claimed there.

In discussing lives of the Celtic Saints it is essential to

remember that most of what we know about them was written in the 11th century, some five hundred years after their time. Fame, cult following and folklore enhanced their attributes, their achievements embellished. Legends grew around them, so that it's often difficult to know where the whole truth lies.

Briefly

B.C.

55	*Roman invasion of Britain – the occupation was to last nearly 500 years, during which time Christianity possibly came via Rome to Britain.*

A.D.

304	*First native Christians martyred at Caerleon.*
341	*Roman Emperor Constantine becomes a Christian.*
410	*Romans leave Britain, the Saxon invasion follows.*
500-600	*Age of the Saints.*
7th Century	*St Augustine meets 7 British Bishops but is rebuffed.*
8th Century	*– acceptance of fusion with Rome and Canterbury.*

part 2

BANGOR cathedral

Maelgwn Gwynedd was the most evil man in Britain, by far the vilest of five such short-listed contemporary rulers in the mid sixth century. So claimed Gildas, the monk, in his extensive sermon, De Exidio Britanniae, as he denounced the corruption and torpidity of the land in his day. In his bid for power Maelgwn had killed his uncle, the king, in a coup d'etat – then in a fit of remorse had taken holy orders. Later he was to murder his wife and nephew in order to marry, in a show of great pomp and splendour, the latter's widow. The ruthless King Maelgwn, it seems, would stop at nothing to achieve his aims. Whether this is a true character assessment may be up for debate, because he appears, whatever his faults, to have been a generous supporter of Christianity. Did Gildas have his own agenda in referring to Maelgwn in such draconian terms? That is an open question.

From his castle at Deganwy, near Conwy, he ruled a great tranche of North Wales and in 546AD invited Deiniol to be Bishop of all my kingdom: hence, unlike all other Celtic sees, Bangor from the start was a territorial diocese.

Deiniol the Blessed, son of King Dunaut of the Northern Pennines, was a saintly man, who with his monks had come to Bangor on the edge of the Menai Straits in 525AD. There he had built the first church, enclosed in a wide area by a wattle fence, in Welsh a 'bangor', in which a mixed community of monks, married and secular clergy and lay families – mainly artisans, tradesmen and agricultural workers – lived together in a community. This was the standard pattern for a Celtic monastery, and gradually from this nucleus grew the present city of Bangor, benefiting from the patronage of the Welsh princes. They provided the security and protection which enabled the monks, in the traditional Celtic fashion, to go out to further evangelise the kingdom and establish daughter churches. While, at the mother church, their leader would provide them with spiritual guidance and encouragement. Celtic saints such as Cybi at Caergybi (Holyhead), Seiriol at Penmon in Anglesey and Cadfan at Tywyn in Gwynedd.

Very little is now known of that early 'cathedral', but an ancient church uncovered at Llandygai, about a mile south of Bangor, may give an indication. This measured 14 feet by 10, and was constructed of vertical posts: could this be a replica of those early cell-like places where the bishops lived, worshipped and gained inspiration to evangelise? Sparse indeed is the evidence; being mostly of wooden construction, little has survived. Like events at the other Welsh Cathedrals little is known of the early times, a period of some 400 years. Professor M.L. Clarke in 'Bangor Cathedral', a book published in 1969, says that it's likely the present cathedral was built on the site of Deiniol's monastery, which was twice sacked, in 634, and again in 1073 by the Vikings. It is following the Norman Conquest in 1066 that the Cathedral story can be really fleshed out.

What with Normans pressing from the east and

native rulers from the south it was unlikely that any rebuilding took place before king of Gwynedd, Gruffudd ap Cynan (c1055-1137), had restored some semblance of order after defeating his enemies. It was during the episcopate of David (the Scott) 1120-39 – Gruffudd's nominee – and with Gruffudd's large financial support that a big cruciform building, 130 feet in length was constructed. He was buried near the high altar.

The earliest reference to a service there is in an account by Giraldus Cambrensis of his tour through Wales in 1188 accompanied by Archbishop Baldwin of Canterbury (Itinerarium Cambria).

Thus a brief summary of the founding of Bangor Fawr yn Arfon, one of the oldest territorial dioceses in the United Kingdom; and Cathedral site: possibly the oldest in continuous and unbroken use.

Deiniol's ancestors migrated to North Wales in the mid fifth century from 'Prydyn in the Old North' – the name given to northern England and southern Scotland – and was a cadet branch member of a royal family. His grandfather Pabo Post Prydyn, a Celtic chieftain, is commemorated at Llanbabo in Anglesey. They and their fellow migrants may well have been converted to Christianity by Ninian, the fifth century Scottish Apostle and his followers.

Deiniol also founded a monastery at Bangor on Dee, which became, according to Bede, the most famous monastery of British Christendom and came to number 2,000 monks before they were routed at the Battle of Chester (c615) by the pagan Aethelfrith, King of

Northumbria. Dr Enid Pierce Roberts asserts that Deiniol and his followers had wandered extensively throughout Wales before arriving at Maelgwn's kingdom in Gwynedd and settled at the eastern entrance to the Menai Straits.

With a fellow bishop, Dyfrig, he was responsible for finally persuading David to take part with them in the memorable Synod of Brefi (c545), an indication of the high respect accorded to Deiniol at this time.

Nothing of Deiniol's church has survived save an indication of the perimeter line around the old 'Bangor' which is still preserved in the Bangor street plan. The old settlement, so it is believed, was on land roughly oval in shape, presently encompassed by the High Street and around Tan y Fynwent to the town clock. John Speed's map of 1610 clearly shows the Cathedral compound apparently little changed from Deiniol's day; it shows the town as a communal settlement, very much smaller than today, all enclosed within an oval perimeter. Here then was where Deiniol established a monastic community with all their little houses and chapel, a small building of wattle and daub, which eventually became the Cathedral. There was no stone church until Gruffudd ap Cynan followed by his son Owain Gwynedd erected a cruciform Norman Church about 130 feet in length early in the 12th century. One round headed window has survived in the south wall of the presbytery. His church had an apsidal (rounded) east end as did the transepts. It had its share of misfortune: in 1210 damaged when King John's men burnt Bangor, but not withstanding, later in the century and during the 14th century considerable building work went on, the Chancel extended and a Lady Chapel created.

In 1402 during the Glyndŵr rebellion, the nave if not the entire Cathedral by one account, was destroyed. An overstatement perhaps, but the nave was certainly open to the elements – for most of the 15th century it was roofless, exposed to the weather, grass grew freely there – 'tir glas fu' ('twas green field there). Never the less Professor M.L. Clarke instances important events taking place in the Cathedral at this time, such as the enthronement of Bishop Nichols in 1409 'with due solemnity and ceremony' and the acquisition of a new font early in the 15th century. So it seems that, in spite of the Cathedral being in a structurally stressed condition, services continued to be held there. By 1533 Bishop Thomas Skeffington in his will directed that '*the steeple and Lofte of Bangor churche where the Bells doo hang be fynished* ...' Under his watch, 1509 to 1533, Bangor Cathedral had undergone several structural changes including building the western tower. Every century since then has seen some developments.

It is also worth recalling that Dr Samuel Johnson and Hester Thrale visited Bangor Cathedral on August 19th 1774. In her diary Mrs Thrale commented that it 'is lighter and better kept in repair than that of St Asaph ... the seats, pulpit etc. are all new ...' Johnson however was not so complimentary in his journal, when they later visited on August 28th: 'We went to worship at the Cathedral. The Quire is mean, the service was not well read' was his rather terse comment. Hester Thrale however on that occasion notes that she 'saw the library, which is not so mean a one as I expected to find'.

So it can be seen that the Cathedral more than held its own through times of adversity.

In taking a look at the furnishings at the crossing, transepts and the presbytery today, it should be noted that they are all Victorian, part of the George Gilbert Scott restoration carried out in the 1870s.

None of the medieval glass has survived. In the 1830s glass was put in the east window, a ten light work designed and created by David Evans of Shrewsbury, but when Gilbert Scott came along he disapproved of it, and relocated those windows in the west end, in the west tower and the two adjoining aisle windows. Gilbert Scott then got Clayton and Bell, a favourite company of his, who had done a great deal of work throughout England and Wales in the second half of the 19th century, to design a window and the beautifully vaulted chancel ceiling. So in the east window there are scenes from the life of our Lord with various Saints from the life of the Church, including one or two Welsh Saints such as David and Deiniol. On the south side of the presbytery we have scenes from the Acts of the Apostles, again by Clayton and Bell.

Gilbert Scott found medieval tiles during his restoration, and he made copies of them, with their symbolic designs, to be incorporated into the chancel floor. Some of the original 14th/15th century tiles can still be seen at the west end of the north aisle. Whilst at the east end, it's worth for a moment to ponder on the magnificent Bishop's throne and canopied stalls, designed by Gilbert Scott and later created by his son Oldrid Scott. The throne was presented to the Cathedral by Sir Watkyn Williams Wynne, PGM on behalf of the Free Masons of the Province of North Wales and Shropshire on May 11th, 1880.

The south transept, the Lady Chapel, is charged with historical interest – here in the southerly wall there is an arched tomb traditionally identified as that of Prince Owain Gwynedd who died in 1170 and Bishop Hywel ap Gronow who died about 1373, but styles and the date of the building of this part of the cathedral, 1275, throws both these possibilities into contention.

Plaques immortalizing two of Wales's pre-eminent bards flank alongside the tomb. Anglesey born Goronwy Owen (1723-69), a Latin scholar at Friars School, Bangor, then briefly at Jesus College, Oxford, as a young man was to revitalize Welsh poetry and give it a new function. Instead of praising patrons he wrote awdlau and cywyddau in the manner of Horace expressing a Christian classicist's reflections on the nature of 'the good life'. But in many ways his desire to enter the priesthood was frustrated, although following a short term teaching posts at Pwllheli, 1742-44, and Denbigh, 1745, he was ordained a deacon in the village of his birth, Llanfair Mathafarn Eithaf; but suffering the poverty of a curate's life had little appeal and he left after a year. Thereafter he led a wandering existence before he was eventually offered a teaching post at a grammar school in Williamsburg, Virginia, which he promptly accepted. Although ultimately his was a hard life often beset by tragedy, his literary legacy to the Welsh nation is immeasurable.

Edmwnd Prys (1544-1623), Priest, Preacher and Poet, a native of Llanrwst and a compatriot of William Morgan (translator of the Bible into Welsh), was Rector of Maentwrog, 1573-1623, and Archdeacon of Merioneth, and is now best remembered for his metrical Psalms, published as an appendix to the Welsh Book of Common Prayer (1621) known as Salmau Cân, the only hymnal used in Wales until the 18th century, and still used in some churches today.

Also on the south wall there's a commemorative plaque to Daniel Silvan Evans (1818-1903) lexicographer, poet, the first Professor of Welsh at the University College of Wales, Aberystwyth (1875-83) and Chancellor of the Cathedral. A native of Llanarth in Cardiganshire, he was ordained a priest in 1849, and served in several North Wales parishes.

In front of the tomb is the altar and lectern: the latter commemorating the life of the eminently ecclesiastic Evan Lewis, Dean of Bangor from 1884 to 1901. South of the altar there's a memorial plaque to J.C. Jones bishop from 1949 to 1956 – 'beloved by all'. The glass in the south window is in memory of H.T. Edwards, Dean from 1876 to 1884; his memorial plaque is on the north side of the altar. The mural above the altar of Christ on his way to Emmaus is by Brian Thomas, probably better known for his stained glass in some London churches, including St Paul's.

The Cathedral was altered in the 1820s, Bangor was growing – it used to be a very small town, but the population grew from the end of the 18th century onwards with the development of the slate quarries. Within the first three decades of the 19th century, the population of Bangor trebled as the slate industry and Porth Penrhyn flourished. The church had to decide how to provide more accommodation – there was talk of building a new church, but there were no funds to do that, so a decision was taken to divide the cathedral into two. A huge screen was built more or less where the altar now stands, east of the screen was fitted out as the cathedral with choir and clergy stalls and seating for the English congregation, while west of the screen was fitted out as the parish church – for the Welsh services, because most of the Bangor inhabitants at that time were Welsh speaking. They removed the medieval crossing arches, so when Gilbert Scott came along in the 1860s, he had to rebuild them. He's often criticised, but he had tremendous regard for the medieval builders – the damage had been done to the fabric of the cathedral before Scott came along. The outer shell of the building was in fair order, but it required a new roof. Scott's verdict on what he found was 'the most execrable gimcrack that ever disgraced a church'. Clearly he faced a tremendous challenge!

The pulpit, designed by Gilbert Scott, is a memorial to Morris Williams (1809-74) better known by his bardic name, Nicander. A native of Llangybi in Gwynedd he is best remembered as a poet, hymnologist, writer and eisteddfodwr. Following curacies at Holywell and

Bangor, he'd held the living of Llanrhuddlad in Anglesey, from 1859 until his death. As one of the group of clergy, members of the Oxford Movement (a High Church movement), who were very good poets and writers, he was very influential in the Bangor diocese. With the clergy from the 1840s onwards came a new breed of men who were very enthusiastic about their work. Among them Evan Lewis, Dean from 1884 to 1901, who assisted in the production of a Welsh Hymn Book and a Welsh Gregorian Psalter; the lectern in the Lady Chapel, presented by his family in 1905, is a fitting tribute his dedication. They were very committed to the church and were responsible for reviving the life of the Church in Wales.

Coming now to the nave altar frontal cover, this is a tapestry depicting facets of life in Gwynedd and was designed and worked by Iris Martin of Celtic Studios, Swansea, in 1975. The base is of white Welsh flannel woven in Ceredigion, the crosses and motives worked in soft leather, gold and lurex threads and several kinds of wool.

The main motif, a large Celtic Cross, is worked in the liturgical green, red, violet and festal gold. The Cross, slightly off-centre, so as not to distract from the High Altar, has set at its centre a small crystal dug from a North Wales mountain.

The tapestry shows aspects of the geography, industry and life of the diocese, featuring mountains, bridges, farming, tourism, Hydro electric and Trawsfynydd Power Stations ...

Nearby, on the left of the pulpit, there's a processional cross which was made by Herr Franz Bonnekamp, an artist in stained glass, who was a prisoner of war in this country. He created it in gratitude for the kindness and care he received at the old C and A Hospital Bangor, when he was seriously ill in 1946. The cross was presented to the City of Bangor on behalf of the twin City of Soest, Germany, and was dedicated by the Dean at a special service on the 30th of June 1980. The Cross was converted to a Processional Cross by the staff of Gwynedd Technical College, Bangor, and was first used at the enthronement of Bishop Cledan Mears on January 8th, 1983.

Two paintings on loan to the Cathedral, displayed in the south aisle, are by Anglesey artist John Granville Gregory. They are a reworking of paintings by Caravaggio of the 17th century in very dramatic contrasting colours , depicting people in contemporary dress: one showing the entombment of Christ, the other Doubting Thomas. They are entitled 'Why' and 'Still Doubting' respectively after 'Entombment' and 'The Incredulity of Saint Thomas' by the Italian old master.

The Mostyn Christ. (mid 15th century), near the west end of the nave, belongs to the Mostyn family, and was entrusted to the custody of the Dean and Chapter of Bangor Cathedral by Lord Mostyn of Mostyn Hall in Clwyd. Carved in oak, almost life-sized, it represents Christ at Calvary before the crucifixion, wearing the crown of thorns. A recusant branch of the Mostyn family remained true to the Catholic faith, and preserved this wonderful medieval carving. Very little medieval woodwork of this kind, known as a Bound Rood, survived the reformation: and may well be the effigy set up in the garden of Rhuddlan Priory in 1518.

At the west end of the north aisle is the 15th century Eva stone. This was discovered on the north side of the chancel during Gilbert Scott's restoration. It's a memorial stone to 'Eva, wife of ... Anwel', fourteenth century. The detail is astonishing, she lies with her head on a pillow. There are 83 buttons on the front of her dress , so detailed you can even see the button holes. She's holding a rosary and various brooches; there are flowers, the inscription is unclear. Near the Eva Stone can be seen the original 14th century tiles with their distinctive Celtic designs, first discovered by Gilbert Scott near the chancel and relocated here in the 1870s.

At the west end of the nave there are two very striking paintings by Brian Thomas originally in the Chapel of St Mary's College in Bangor. (St Mary's was a church college of education closely linked with Bangor and St Asaph dioceses; generations of teachers were taught their skills there; it closed about 1980). One portrays the six Welsh cathedrals, on a relief map of Wales indicating their locations, the other shows some of the important people connected with the Church in Wales, especially those who contributed to education: St Dyfrig, St Illtyd, Gruffudd Jones Llanddowror, Bishop William Morgan, John Davies Mallwyd, and many others.

Music at Bangor Cathedral

It appears that music featured early at Bangor because we have a poem by Dafydd ap Gwilym, the most distinguished of Welsh medieval poets, addressed to the Dean, Hywel ap Gronow some time before 1370, which says of the cathedral – 'ty geirwgalch teg ei organ' ('a house white-washed as white as foam, fair is its organ'). This tells us not only that the Cathedral was in use at this early date but also something about its appearance, gleaming white, and that it had a fine instrument for choral accompaniment.

And further 'as for the choir, there is no one who can be compared to them', the poet said. There is also reference to an organ in a poem by Anglesey poet Gruffudd Gryg, a contemporary of Dafydd ap Gwilym, who witnessed the arrival of a new instrument (between 1350 and 1370) and tells of how all the parishioners contributed towards it.

During the episcopate of Bishop Henry Rowlands (1598-1616) arrangements were made for the payment of a stipend to an organist, but during the tenure of his successor Bishop Lewis Bayly we hear of one organist, Thomas Bolton, complaining that he had not received his salary!

The next musical reference is in relation to the Bangor Grammar School, known as 'Friars', so named after the 13th century Friary (Black Friars), the site of the school when it was first established in 1557. In his will the school's founder Geoffrey Glyn provided for ten poor scholars to receive the sum of £2 annually, and directed them under the school's statutes to attend the Cathedral wearing surplices on Sunday. By 1691 we find that Friars scholars who sang in the cathedral would be called 'singing boys' and paid from Cathedral funds. They practised on Thursdays and Saturdays, receiving the rest of their education at Friars School pursuing courses in Latin and Greek as laid down by Elizabethan statutes.

During the Commonwealth 1649-1660 the organ was either removed or destroyed in accordance with the parliamentary order 'for the speedy demolition of all organs, images, and all matters of superstitious monuments in all cathedrals ... throughout the kingdom of England and the dominion of Wales'.

When Charles II was restored to the throne in 1660 a new organ was installed, paid from a legacy of £100 left by Bishop William Roberts and erected by his successor, Robert Morgan; on the organ case was a Latin verse in which the two bishops, who had provided the money and erected the organ, were compared to David and Solomon respectively.

In 1779 the organ was replaced by a new instrument. It cost three hundred and sixty guineas and was made by Samuel Green, the leading organ builder of his day. This was in constant use until it was replaced by the present organ which was built by one of the greatest master organ builders of the 19th century – William Hill – and installed in 1873.

The organ was completely re-planned and reconstructed in 1954 by the John Compton Organ Company Ltd of London, the Great Swell and Pedal organs brought out of the organ chamber and re-erected in the North Transept by David Wells of Liverpool, where their tone was unobstructed and access for tuning greatly improved.

The Solo Organ speaks through the western arch of the organ chamber, the Choir Organ through the south west arch, while the detached new console placed in the north Transept enables the organist to hear the organ, choir and congregation in proper proportion.

As expected in an area with a fine choral tradition together with a great centre of musical resource at its university, Bangor's musical reputation is the envy of north west Wales. Of its Organists in the twentieth century, probably the best known and longest serving was Bangor born Dr Leslie Douglas Paul; a memorial inscription in the Cathedral reads:

'In memory of Leslie Paul, D.Mus. F.R.C.O. F.R.A.M.
Organist and Master of the Choristers, 1927-1969
Given by friends and former choristers'

Following his retirement – Leslie Paul died in 1970 – he was followed by Anglesey born John Hywel who had studied the organ with Dr Leslie Paul and later became Head of the Music Department at Bangor University. But due to pressure of work resigned as Cathedral Choirmaster in July 1971. He was succeeded by Andrew Goodwin who had served as organ scholar at the Cathedral under John Hywel. A Middlesex man, he had previously gained his honours degree in music at

Liverpool University and had studied the organ with the eminent Dr Caleb Jarvis. His tenure as organist and choir-master (while also fulfilling duties as part time organ tutor at the University and examiner to the Associated Board of the Royal Schools of Music) continued until 2003 when the mantle of Acting Musical Director was taken on by Graham Eccles who was formerly Musical Director at St Asaph Cathedral. Mr Eccles first studied the organ at Worksop College where he gained his LTCL and ARCO diplomas, and subsequently at the Royal Northern College of Music under Robert Frost, with master classes conducted by Dame Gillian Weir, Thomas Trotter and Nigel Alcoat. Upon leaving the Royal Northern College of Music he was awarded the Graduate Diploma and Professional Performance Diploma, also the ARCM and FRCO Diplomas.

Starting in 1989 as Assistant Organist at Chester Cathedral, he went on to St Asaph in 1998.

Over in Bangor the high standards of musical excellence are maintained under his watch. A popular accompanist and recitalist, his credits include performing with the Halle and Royal Liverpool Philharmonic Orchestras at the Proms in London.

Questioned on his role in Bangor, he'll admit that as a freelancer his main income is from giving recitals, teaching, examining, orchestral work and with choral societies. He lives in St Asaph and goes over to Bangor four times a week, 'its a question of fitting everything in', he says. During term time, especially, he'll need to go sometimes to Manchester or Liverpool – lots of miles in a week. 'I'm enjoying it' he says 'but there's a lot of work to do, not least in recruitment of boys for the Cathedral Choir. I want to sort that out and establish a separate girls choir as well'. Having a separate girls' choir would give greater flexibility and provide more groups to perform in the diocese – more resources.

So how does he do the recruiting? 'I visit schools, get leaflets printed and distributed, make contact with music teachers, people in choirs, the William Mathias Music Centre at the Galeri in Caernarfon, try and make friends with these people. I'm focusing on church schools in the area. Its taking a long time, relationships need building up. I need to think of new ways of enlisting people. In the old days in a cathedral congregation, you'd have families there. There are no children in the Cathedral congregation on a Sunday morning to draw from for the choir. This isn't just a local problem, its the same in lots of places unfortunately. So I've got to look outside'.

Giving six-seven year old children Cathedral experience, getting them acquainted with the cathedral is part of his strategy. It includes a singing session at the Cathedral; at the end of the day, everyone has had a great time everything is lovely – 'I could easily make a cathedral choir from that lot. We ask, did you enjoy that? Yes, all hands go up! But getting them there on recruitment day is a different matter. I'm still working on how we can do this. Of course there has to be parental commitment. Four sessions a week is quite an undertaking but the rewards are tremendous'.

So how does he quantify them? 'Apart from the

church aspect of it – the religious education; its a musical education, the regular disciplined work for the music in the service gives them a sense of purpose and dignity, their reading improves immensely – with having to sing the psalms, reading comes naturally. Some play musical instruments too, and given time some just take it on board, due to the amount of music they have to get through in a week – I try out new pieces so it keeps it fresh and interesting. It becomes a production line and they find how to learn quickly, efficiently and they get on with it. It prepares them well for later life. At schools, teachers comment on how much their reading improves as a result of being in the choir. Lots of choristers look back on their time with great fondness'.

In his quest at Bangor he's ably aided by Martin Brown the assistant organist, who plays the organ while Eccles conducts the choir. He gives him due credit: 'Martin Brown is a good chap, he's been there since he left university; he's incredible – he's the assistant organist, chapter clerk, cathedral administrator – and he's part time! In other words, working for The Dean and Chapter he runs the place, down to producing the order of service each week, he lives for the place'.

So what of rehearsal times? 'Tuesday is rehearsal with the boys for evensong, Thursday with the boys and lay clerks, then the men stay on for an hour rehearsing for next week and on Friday rehearsing for the service on Sunday morning for the Eucharist. They then do rehearsal for evensong. The boys usually come at four o'clock and the weekday services are 5.30. for about forty minutes. Once they get interested in doing it, you find new boys think , this is a lot of work – 'Do I really want to do this?', but you can see that they do and there's a little resistance, but once they get over that they really start enjoying it, you just can't keep them away! They love it because otherwise they wouldn't come, they get a bit of pocket money every half term – but they don't come just because of that. The pocket money is just a bit of encouragement and people give them chocolates at Christmas, Easter and whatever, they do it because they get something out of it.

Often there are very few worshipers at evensong, its almost like it might have been in monastic times, doing it for the worship – not singing to a congregation. At other times they're singing to a full cathedral which is great, a large congregation doesn't faze them at all, they don't seem to get nervous, some of the boys will even sing solos.

The choristers join the choir at about seven years old and they carry on until their voices break – but people tell me that fifty years ago people's voices broke later. Its funny, voices seem to break in different ways, some just drift down in pitch bit by bit others just crack and make an awe-full noise. Some then leave and come back later. Being in a choir helps them for when their voices mature'.

'When we get a girls choir it'll be easier, they will stay until school-leaving age. By the time they're 17 or 18, they're young professionals in a way. They will have gained more experience – there are some fabulous girls' choirs about. Girls who have sung in the cathedral previously were excellent, there's great potential out there. Some girls have brothers, so there could be a spin-off. Its gently does it, and if we get to do it we've got to do it properly and really make it work. We could share out the services, the boys could do their part and the girls could fill in to provide more flexibility. The boys could have a week-end off and the girls in turn could have theirs. This would be more attractive for people if they want a week-end away or something. If this can be accommodated without jeopardising the cathedral music, that's all to the good.

We also have ten men ('lay clerks') at the moment. One or two studying at the university as well, tenor, bass … whatever and that can be helpful, but of course at Christmas and Easter, these students will have gone home. Its good to incorporate them while they are here however. We've just been donated a harpsichord by a local choir that wasn't using it very much, they gifted it to the cathedral. The harpsichord is lovely and the organ was restored three years ago by David Wells of Liverpool, its magnificent now. We have things going on at lunch times, organ recitals and so on and people are invited in. The University use the cathedral as a venue as well, this is a link that we want to build up a bit more. Professor John Harper is the head of church music at the University; their church music course is known worldwide where students can study to quite a high standard. I have some research students there who we like to get involved in some sort of way'.

At the time of writing this book (early 2011) Graham Eccles was busily preparing the choir for a special service on Sunday February 6th 2011 to celebrate the digitalisation of one of the Cathedral's most treasured volumes, 'Bishop Anian's Pontifical', otherwise known as the 'Bangor Pontifical', a book which belonged to Bishop Anian 2 (1309-28). Its a book containing the services which only a bishop can perform such as Confirmation, Ordination and Consecration of Churches, written on vellum, rubricated (with headings) in red and blue, with illuminations inlaid with gold leaf and bordered in blue, green and black. Almost everything that was necessary for a bishop's public duties including appropriate music, written in the standard notation of the day is contained within its pages. 'Its plain song music is peculiar to Bangor, so that's going to be really interesting. It goes back to monastic times again, I'm looking at that as a resource to treasure', says Graham Eccles.

And the wonder is that for over 700 years the 'Pontifical' has survived at all; enduring Bangor's at times tumultuous history, warlike skirmishes and the Owain Glyndŵr rebellion in 1402, when for a time it was lost. Returned to the Cathedral in 1485 by Bishop Richard Ednam and later somehow finding private refuge when threatened with destruction when Roman service books were banned, the Pontifical surfaced in 1701 when it was presented to the Cathedral by Bishop Humphrey Humphreys.

During World War 2 it was kept safely in the tunnels under the National Library of Wales at Aberystwyth, and finally returned to Bangor on 11th April 1946.

The Bishop and Dean

The Bishop of Bangor Cathedral, The Rt Revd Andrew John is a native of Aberystwyth and was elected Bishop of Bangor in October 2008. He was educated at Ysgol Penglais before reading Law at the University of Wales, Cardiff. Following his graduation in 1986, he went on to study theology at the University of Nottingham. After graduating there in 1988, he studied for his diploma in Pastoral Studies at St John's College Nottingham following which he was ordained a deacon in the Diocese of St David's and in 1990, a priest. All his ministry prior to coming to Bangor was in that diocese, firstly as curate of Cardigan, Y Ferwig, and Mwnt from 1989 to 1991, then Aberystwyth 1991 to 1992 before becoming a vicar in the Rectorial Benefice there from 1992 to 1999.

He was vicar of Henfynwy with Aberaeron & Llandewi Aberarth, to which was added Llanbadarn Trefeglwys in 2005. In 2006 appointed vicar of Pencarreg & Llwynycrwys, and Archdeacon of Cardigan.

Married to Caroline who was herself ordained a Deacon at the same service during which her husband became a priest, they have four children: son Matt and daughters Bethany, Hannah and Harriet.

The Dean of Bangor Cathedral from 2004 to 2011 was The Very Revd Alun John Hawkins. Born in 1944, educated at King's College London, he lectured in English and Drama at the University College of North Wales Bangor until his ordination in 1981. Following a curacy at Dwygyfylchi, he became Rector of Llanberis and then Vicar of Knighton and Norton.

Prior to his Deanery appointment, he was from 1993 Canon Residentiary at Bangor Cathedral and Archdeacon of Bangor from 2000.

Dean Alun Hawkins retired in July 2011.

The Dean of Bangor Cathedral, formerly Residentiary Canon Missioner Revd Dr Sue Jones took up her appointment on August 1st 2011. Born in Barry, South Wales she started her career working for the Midland Bank before training as a teacher in Trinity College Carmarthen.

She was called to the ministry in 1993 and received her training in Rippon College and ordained a Deacon in 1995 at Brecon Cathedral – one of the first women priests to be ordained there.

Her first appointment was as Chaplain at Swansea University, moving to St Michael's College Llandaff in 1998 as Director of Studies. In 2000 she moved to the Bangor Diocese to pioneer and develop theological study across the diocese. This became known as 'Exploring Faith' which was run under the Ministry Course at Bangor. It is now called the St Seiriol Centre which has responsibility for training people for ministry in the Diocese.

During this period she was also vicar in the Parish of Bangor with special responsibility for St Peter's church in Penrhosgarnedd as well as being the Area Dean for Ogwen and Canon of Bangor Cathedral.

Bangor Cathedral

Bishop of Bangor: The Rt Revd Andrew John.
Dean of Bangor: The Very Revd Dr Sue Jones.
Succentor: The Revd Michael Outram.
Director of Music: Mr Graham Eccles.
Assistant Organist: Mr Martin J. Brown.
Chapter Clerk and Administrator: Mr Martin J Brown. Telephone: (01248) 353 983
e-mail: cathedral.bangor@gmail.com
Website: www.churchinwales.org.uk and click on the link to Bangor Diocese.

Times of Services

Sundays:

8.00am	Holy Communion
9.45am	Cymun Bendigaid
11.00am	Choral Eucharist
3.15pm	Choral Evensong

Monday to Friday:

10.30am	Eucharist
5.30pm	Choral Evensong Tuesday and Thursday (in school term time)

Bishops

c.546-572	Deiniol
572-c.775	*Dates & names for this period are not known*
c.775-809	Elfodd
809-c.904	*Dates & names for this period are not known*
c.904-44	Morlais
944-c.1050	*Dates & names for this period are not known*
c.1050- ?	Dyfan
c.1081- ?	Revedun
1092-1108	Hervey le Breton
1109-20	*See vacant*
1120-39	David the Scot
1140-61	Meurig
c.1163-69	(*Arthur of Bardsey*)
1177-c.1190	Gwion
el.c.1193/96	(*Rotoland*)
1195-96	Alan
1197-1213	Robert of Shrewsbury
1215-36	Cadwgan of Llandyfai
1236	(*Hywel ap Ednyfed*)
1236-1267	Richard
1267-1307	Enion
1307-09	Gruffydd ap Iorwerth
1309-28	Einion Sais
1328-57	Matthew de Englefeld
1357	(*Ithel ap Robert*)
1357-66	Thomas de Ringstead O.P.
1366	(*Alexander Dalby*)
1366-70	Gervase de Castro O.P.
1371-72	Hywel ab Goronwy

1372-75	John Gilbert O.P.
c.1375/76	(*Geoffrey Herdeby O.F.S.A.*)
1376-98	John Swaffham O.Cist
1398	(*Lewis Aber*)
1398-1404	Richard Young
1405-08	(*Lewis Byford*)
1408-18	(*Griffin Young*)
1408-17	Benedict Nichols
1418-23	William Barrow
1423-35	John Clederowe
1436-48	Thomas Cheriton O.P.
1448-53	John Stanberry O.P.
1453-64	James Blakedon O.P.
1464-94	Richard Edenham O.F.M.
1494-1500	Henry Deane O.Can.S.A.
1500-04	Thomas Pigot O.S.B.
1504-08	John Penny O.Can.S.A.
1509-33	Thomas Skevington O.Cist.
1534-39	John Capon O.S.B.
1539-41	John Bird O.Carm.
1541-52	Arthur Bulkeley
1552-58	*See Vacant*
1555-58	William Glyn
1558	(*Maurice Clenock*)
1559-66	Rowland Meyrick
1566-85	Nicholas Robinson
1586-95	Hugh Bellot
1596-97	Richard Vaughan
1598-1616	Henry Rowlands
1616-31	Lewis Bayly
1632-33	David Dolben

1634-37	Edmund Griffith
1637-65	William Roberts
1665-66	Robert Price
1666-73	Robert Morgan
1673-89	Humphrey Lloyd
1689-1701	Humphrey Humphreys
1701-16	John Evans
1715-21	Benjamin Hoadly
1721-23	Richard Reynolds
1723-27	William Baker
1728-34	Thomas Sherlock
1734-37	Charles Cecil
1737-43	Thomas Herring
1743-47	Mathew Hutton
1748-56	Zachary Pearce
1756-68	John Egerton
1769-74	John Ewer
1774-83	John Moore
1783-1800	John Warren
1800-06	William Cleaver
1807-09	John Randolph
1809-30	Henry Majendie
1830-59	Christopher Bethell
1859-90	Colquhoun Campbell
1890-98	Lewis Lloyd
1899-1924	Watkin Williams
1925-28	Daniel Davies
1928-44	Charles Green
1944-48	David Edwardes Davies
1949-56	John Jones
1957-82	Gwilym Williams

1982-92	Cledan Mears
1993-99	Barry Morgan
2000-04	Saunders Davies
2004-08	Anthony Crockett
2008-	Andrew John

Deans

1162	Arthur de Bardsey
1236	Guy
1254	William
1286	Kyndelw
1328	Adam
1371	Hywel ap Goronwy
1371-1382	John Martyn
1389	Walter de Swaffham
1396	William Clyve
1397	David Daron
1410	William Pollard
1410	Henry Honore
1413-1416	Roger Wodele
1423-1436	Nigel Bondeby
1445	John Martin
1464	Hugh Alcock
1468	Huw Morgan
1480-1502	Richard Cyffin
1502	David Yale
1503	Richard Cowland
1509-1534	John Glynne
1534-1554	Robert Evans

1554	Rhys Powell
1557	Robert Evans
1570	Roland Thomas
1583	Henry Rowlands
1588-1593	Held by the Bishop in Commendam
1599-1604	Richard Parry
1605	John Williams
1613	Edmund Griffith
1634	Griffith Williams
1672	William Lloyd
1680	Humphrey Humphreys
1689	John Jones
1727	Peter Maurice
1750	Hughe Hughes
1753	Thomas Lloyd
1793	John Warran
1838	James Henry Cotton
1862-76	James Vincent Vincent
1876-84	Henry Thomas Edwards
1884-1901	Evan Lewis
1902-03	John Pryce
1903	Griffith Roberts
1934-40	Henry Lewis James
1940	Thomas Alfred Edwards
1941	John Thomas Davies
1955	John Richard Richards
1957	Hywel Islwyn Williams
1962	Gwynfryn Richards
1971	Benjamin Noel Young Vaughan
1976	John Ivor Rees
1988-1998	Thomas Erwyd Prys Edwards

1998-2003	Trevor Evans
2004-July 2011	Alun Hawkins
September 2011	Susan Helen Jones

Organists

1644	Thomas Bolton
1689	(A Vicar Choral) ?
1691	Thomas Roberts
1705	? Priest
1708	? Smith
1710	? Ferrer
1713	John Rathbone
1721	Thomas Rathbone
1750	Thomas Lloyd
1778	Richard Jarred
1782	William Shrubsole
1784	Edmun Olive
1793	Joseph Pring
1842	James Sharpe Pring
1868	Robert Roberts
1872	Roland Rogers
1892	T. Westlake Morgan
1906	Roland Rogers (reappointed)
1928	Leslie Douglas Paul
1956-62	David Gwerfyl Davies
1970	John Hywel
1972	Andrew John Goodwin
2009-	Graham Eccles

Sources

The Cathedral Church of St Deiniol Bangor (Pitkin Guide).

Bangor Cathedral by M.L. Clarke (University of Wales Press, Cardiff 1969).

The Organists and Organs of the Welsh Cathedrals in the 20th Century. Compiled by Enid Bird.

A Grand Tour of North Wales by Meurig Owen, Gwasg Carreg Gwalch, Llanrwst (2003).

'Cydymaith i Lenyddiaeth Cymru' Gol. Meic Stephens, Gwasg Prifysgol Cymru Caerdydd (1997).

Bangor Cathedral Website.

Acknowledgements

David Price (interview 20.1.2011)
Graham Eccles (interview 17.1.2011)

Brecon Cathedral

The site of Brecon Cathedral has a history which probably goes back to the 5th and 6th century 'age of the Saints', but it was only in 1923 that it became the Cathedral Church of the newly founded Diocese of Swansea and Brecon. Since 1538, when monasteries were suppressed by Henry V111, it had served the community as a Parish Church.

And for some 500 years before that it was a Benedictine Priory, first established as such in the wake of the Norman Conquest. It was founded in 1093 by Bernard de Neufmarche following his defeat of Rhys ap Tewdwr, king of Brycheiniog at Brecon. Bernard gave the 'church of St John the Evangelist near his castle of Brecon' together with 'a certain property called the Old Town' (which may refer to the Roman Fort – Brecon Gaer), to the newly founded Benedictine Abbey of Battle in Sussex.

It was in Battle that William the Conqueror fought against Harold in a bitter and bloody war to assume control of England in 1066, the infamous Battle of Hastings. William had made a vow in an Abbey at St Valerie Sur Somme, before the sea crossing, in which he promised to establish a monastery free of episcopal control if God granted him victory. According to the 'Chronicles of Battel Abbey (which date from about 1180), the Abbey was 'founded by the Conqueror in expiation for the sin involved in the conquest'. Upon his death he left many gifts to the Abbey, which meant that it became one of the wealthiest religious houses in the

47

country. So we learn (from the Chronicle) that Roger, a monk there – Bernard's confessor , a prime mover in the priory's development at Brecon, undertook the rebuilding of the church 'from its foundations' and added domestic buildings. Thus it became a cell of Battle Abbey until its dissolution. Much of the present Brecon Cathedral dates from this period and in an Architectural Study entitled 'The Cathedral Church of St John The Evangelist Brecon' (published by the 'Friends of Brecon Cathedral' in 1994 to mark the 900th Anniversary of the Foundation) a well illustrated historical record is given.

Very little historical detail pre-dates this, although the early Celtic Saints and their monastic traditions once held sway here. A nearby Roman road and formidable fort, Y Gaer, built in AD 75; covering an area of 6.5 acres, one of the largest of its kind in Wales, with its complement of Spanish soldiers is an indication of possible avenues by which Christianity reached these parts. By 341 AD the Emperor Constantine was a convert and Christianity had become an acceptable religion within the Roman Empire, of which Wales was a part. Much of the culture of 6th century saints, living a monastic life which originated in Egypt – like that at St Asaph – could have flourished here. Saints like the learned Illtud, an abbot at Llantwit Major, was a great influence training men at his monastery, which spawned similar communities throughout South Wales and Brittany.

Rod Cooper in his admirable 'Abbeys and Priories of Wales' published in 1993, described their ascetic way of life: 'One group of unskilled members of the community would be set to labour on the land, another group to labour in the monastery. Those fitted for maintaining worship of the church were mainly confined to the monastery for that purpose although some would be engaged in the missionary work that was an important aspect of most communities. These communities, in their remote settings and with the most primitive buildings have left no survivals except a few carved stones and crosses. But in the Welsh mind those early ideals survived and even in the Norman period the hermit's life was respected and commonly sought after'. As he mentions, very little has survived from before the 11th century; the unsettled nature of the Welsh meant their structures were mainly of wood. It was after the Norman Conquest that we see buildings of stone and a rather different church regime developing. The present Dean of Brecon, the Very Reverend Geoffrey Marshall believes that a Celtic Church once stood on the Cathedral site and points out its circular boundary, a feature of Celtic times, as evidence to support his assertion. It is interesting to surmise the scene back in the early Norman days when Roger, the Benedictine monk, set about rebuilding the church from its foundations; dismantling the former wooden structure to be replaced by a magnificent stone edifice. Much of what is known of the Celtic saints was written in the 12th century by Norman clerks here at Brecon Priory.

Brecon Cathedral is sited on an elevated position overlooking the town, north west of the River Honddu. Built of locally quarried stone and well grown seasoned timber from within the area, it can justifiably claim to be 'the finest ecclesiastical edifice in Wales'. In its priory days it was used as a parish church: the people of Brecon worshipped in the nave, while the monastery used the rest of the building. From at least 1408 it was known as the church of the Holy Rood or Holy Cross. A popular place of pilgrimage in the late 15th and early 16th century when people were drawn there by the great Golden Rood (Cross) before its destruction at the Dissolution. Known in Welsh as 'Crôg Aberhonddu', it was credited with miraculous healing properties and medieval poets would compose their 'cywyddau' (poems in a special metre) as tributes to it.

The priory was endowed with property and land around Brecon, together with several churches and grange-farms in Wales and the borders. Until the mid 13th century successive Lords of Brecknock and their major feudal tenants added to its land holdings, notably William de Breos (d.1211) sheriff of Herefordshire. A stained glass commemorative window on the North Wall (left of the main Cathedral doorway) represents a memorial to three great families which held the Lordship of Brecknock at this time: Giles de Breos Bishop of Hereford (d.1215) – centre – with to his left Humphrey de Bohun (related through marriage to de Breos) and Anne, Countess of Stafford (right).

The number of monks (apart from the Prior) was never more than 6; in 1401 only 4 and in 1435 and 1535 there were 5. The Prior was of considerable local importance; he would normally control and administer the whole estate. He was appointed by the Abbot of Battle Abbey and could be called to the mother house at will. At least two, Prior Reginald, (1248-60) and Prior William Westfield, (1497-1503), themselves became Abbots of Battle.

In addition to the monks there were a larger number of servants which included a janitor and steward; in 1535 there were 15. They insulated the priory from the town, although at the priory church they would impinge upon one another, (the nave of which was the parish church of Brecon – St Mary's being a chapel of ease: it became a parish church when the priory became a Cathedral in 1923); monks from the priory were expected to assist the parish priest.

At the dissolution (1538) by Thomas Cromwell, vicar-general and deputy to King Henry VIIIth as head of the church, everything of value from the priory was sold by the Crown and the property leased out to Sir John Price of Breconshire, a relative through marriage of Thomas Cromwell. His descendant Richard Price acquired the rest of the buildings in 1576 and took over maintaining the chancel. In the dispersal, ownership of the five bells in the tower, two large ones which belonged to the priory and the three smaller, were in dispute. In the Crown Commissioner's valuation, someone had made a bid to buy the three smaller bells as well. A plea by the parishioners that the three smaller bells belonged to them was upheld by the Royal Commissioners and so there they remained until replaced in the 18th century.

By the beginning of the 19th century the structure had gone into severe decline, its internal chapels ruinous, windows boarded, only the nave was used for regular services.

In 1836 Lord Camden paid for re-slating the chancel, and a screen was put between the nave and crossing in an attempt to make the building more usable. Further serious restoration was undertaken in 1860. Following a report by Gilbert Scott, in 1860-62 the east end was restored at a cost of approximately £2,700 and from 1872 further costs of about £5,600 were incurred restoring the nave and aisles. The 20th century saw further remedial work carried out including strengthening the tower which was threatening to split and collapse. And again at the beginning of the 21st century work was carried out to combat rising damp which was putting the church fabric in jeopardy. Rather surprisingly, removing the plaster improved the Cathedral's acoustics.

By 1860 the priory church was being put forward as the natural choice for the cathedral of a diocese of Central Wales thus subdividing the diocese of St Davids, which was then the largest in England and Wales. In 1890 there were firm proposals for a new diocese for Swansea and Brecon, but by then ideas for the Welsh Church disestablishment were also under consideration. In the event both matters came to a resolution: Welsh Church disestablishment came about in 1920 with the new Swansea and Brecon Diocese in 1923.

Part of the history since 1923 must be the Regimental Chapel which is housed in the Havard Chapel. This is a reminder of the Cathedral's links with the town and its long time military association. This began, according to cathedral warden Lieut. Col. Rodney Ashwood, in 1873 when the 24th South Wales Borderers Regiment opened its barracks in Brecon. In 1879 the Regiment went out to fight in the Zulu wars: such was the impact that memorials were erected to them. After World War 1, the Borderers decided that they should have a memorial inside the Cathedral. So this led in 1923 to the Havard Chapel (or Vicars Chapel) being given over to them as their Regimental Chapel. (The Havard Chapel was originally erected by the Havard family of Pontwylim, a local family of great influence in the 14th century, and as a memorial to Sir Walter Havard (Havre de Grace), a Norman knight of the 11th century – one of the 12 knights of Baron de Neufmark. Other knights included Sir Reginald Newbury, who married Sir Walter's daughter. Both the Havards and the Aubreys were prominent Brecon families for many years). The Chapel now known as that of the Prince of Wales' Own South Wales Borderers is full of regimental memorabilia; plaques on the seats – in memoriam, regimental colours once lost – then recovered during the Zulu War and a tributary wreath placed by Queen Victoria are on honourable display here. A 1914-18 War Memorial plaque records how '311 officers and 5,466 men of the South Wales Borderers 24th Regiment gave their lives in the Great War; and this Havard Chapel has been beautified by their comrades and friends in proud and grateful thanksgiving'. A glass cabinet on the north wall contains two Rolls of Honour, in handsome book form, giving the names of the fallen in both World Wars, including 96 officers and 946 men in the 1939-45 War. Rodney Ashwood says that in 1969 the regiment became the Royal Regiment of Wales with a further designated chapel in Llandaff Cathedral, which is now the main one. But the Brecon Chapel has many visitors and prayers are said there regularly, as is a weekly service of Holy Communion.

Music at Brecon Cathedral

'**Music features strongly** here' says Rodney Ashwood, 'it's even a strong component of the famous Brecon Jazz Festival when the Cathedral is packed out in a service of hymn singing to jazz accompaniment'.

The present Musical Director Mark Duthie (here since 2007) and assistant Meirion Wyn Jones perpetuate the strong musical Brecon heritage. They followed a remarkable husband and wife team, David Gedge and Hazel Davies who served for forty one years and wrote 'A Country Cathedral Organist Looks Back' (2005) and 'More from a Country Cathedral Organist' (2008)', a detailed account of musical life in Brecon.

In May 1948 the first Archdeaconry of Brecon Choral Festival was held at the Cathedral and continued on an annual basis until Humphrey Carden retired in May 1956 after a tenure of 33 years. Born in Dunbartonshire, in 1886 Mr Carden was educated at Hereford Cathedral. He married a Herefordshire lady, a violinist who had played in a string quartet with Edward Elgar. A keen sportsman, he could get his young choristers on board and enthuse them and he's spoken of as a great force for good. He was followed by Dowlais born (1913), D.

Gwerfyl Davies who initiated a series of organ recitals after Evensong on Sundays. He also organised a special service sung by the combined choirs of the Cathedral and Christ College along with those of St David's and St Mary's Churches Brecon on the Festival of St Luke the Evangelist, October 18, 1958.

Dr Gwerfyl Davies remained at Brecon until 1962, leaving, upon his appointment as Music Advisor to the Leicester Education Committee.

Upon Bryan Hesford's appointment in 1963, weekday Choral Evensong was restored, using for the first time, musical settings of the canticles which were brought into regular use at Cathedral services. This led to an invitation from the BBC to broadcast Choral Evensong. In addition to his organist's duties, Manchester born Bryan Hesford was a Senior Examiner at the Trinity College of Music London from 1967-85, Editor of the Musical Opinion 1976-85 and Editor of The Organ from 1976-80 as well as a very active composer.

London born (1939) David Gedge's appointment in 1966 signalled a series of annual Summer recitals leading to a 'Songs of Praise' broadcast from the town. Also initiating a Christmas Carol Concert as an annual event at St Mary's. It is clear that during his tenure, a bewildering amount of music-making took place with frequent choral and orchestral concerts by visiting choirs and musicians. These included eminent recitalists such as Dr Francis Jackson, Organist at York Minster and Christopher Dearnley of St Paul's Cathedral, many of these events broadcast. The Brecon Cathedral Choir went out to sing in other cathedrals too: St David's, St

Asaph, Hereford, Worcester, Lincoln, Sheffield and St Paul's and in the 1970s toured Canada, USA, Germany, Denmark and Ireland. David Gedge was a dedicated musician, a human dynamo – an extrovert who could influence and persuade; often able to round up the most unlikely lads into the Cathedral choir.

1979 saw inauguration of the custom of giving the major festivals, Christmas, Easter and Whitsun a particular musical prominence. In that year a Good Friday performance by Gwent Chamber Orchestra of Bach's Harpsichord Concerto in F minor with soloist Hugh Thomas followed on Holy Saturday with a performance of The Messiah by the Cathedral Singers and the orchestra. And at the close of the year J.S.Bach Cantatas sung at Sunday Evensongs during Advent (sung with soloists and orchestral accompaniment) and a Viennese Mass-Setting at Holy Eucharist on Christmas Day.

In 1980 the Cathedral Choir formed part of a massed choir of 2,000 voices that led the singing at Celebration 80, a great Holy Eucharist service in the National Stadium Cardiff to commemorate the diamond jubilee of The Church in Wales. David Gedge conducted the combined choir while his wife Hazel Davies, played an electronic organ which had been especially installed for the occasion.

David Gedge who was Head of Music at Builth Wells High School from 1966, formed the Cathedral Singers in that year, and in 1975 established the Gwent Chamber Orchestra, retiring in 2007. He was a widely published writer and gave lectures for the W.E.A. and University College Cardiff Extra Mural Department.

In 2002 a decision was taken to set up an endowment fund of £1,000,000 to secure a sound financial basis for music at Brecon Cathedral to which H.R.H. Prince Charles agreed to be Patron. By 2010 about £750,000 had been raised. Archbishop Rowan Williams gave his full backing at an event at Lambeth Palace in 2008 in which the Brecon Choristers sang, to which the London Welsh community were invited. A grant of £40,000 by 'Friends of Cathedral Music' made in 2009 was a further boost. All of which was very encouraging to Music Director Mark Duthie and his Assistant Organist Meirion Wyn Jones who both took up duties in 2007. When the new dioceses were formed in the 1920s there wasn't much money about and up to quite recently its been 'quite tough to pay for a Musical Director and Assistant; unlike many English Cathedrals we don't have properties we can rent out or stocks and shares'.

'The instrumental and singing lessons for the choristers, and their general musical education is the main purpose of the Trust Fund' explains Meirion Wynn Jones. The choristers number 26 both boys and girls in equal numbers all aged between 8 and 13. The girls leave the choir at the same age as boys naturally do and both may go on to join the Cathedral Consort, a newly formed mixed chamber choir. In addition, the Cathedral Choir consists of 11 lay clerks, some of whom come from quite a distance – as far as Bristol and Neath.

Recruiting in a sparsely populated area like mid Wales is challenging and the youngsters are mainly drawn from about eight schools around Brecon. Mark Duthie and Meirion Wyn Jones will go out to the schools and invite 7 and 8 year olds to join in groups and play games with them, singing and clapping 'to see what they've got'. They will then make a selection to come for a trial audition to find out if the promise is there. 'We make the commitment clear to the parents from from the outset, when we invite a selection of children to apply for an audition' says Mark Duthie. The rehearsal timetable takes place as follows: Wednesday: 4.15-5.45pm; Thursday 4.15-5.45pm. (Followed by Treble voices Evensong at least once a month). Friday: 4.15pm, Evensong 5.45 followed by rehearsal for Sunday morning until 7pm. Sunday: Services at 11am and 3.30pm, each preceded by Choir Practice, 'so its a serious commitment, impacting on siblings and the family as a whole'. The practices are held in a song-room upstairs, an old monastic bedroom. New choristers will be trained in the theory of music and taught how to read it. Its an exercise that gives them confidence and shows them how to be team players. Meirion Wyn Jones, who is a professional piano and organ teacher, will give some of them lessons, while the Trust pays for lessons given by a large number of local teachers paid out of the Cathedral fund. It may sound like a stiff regime but they have a lot of fun too: as soon as they come to the practices they get toast, jam and squash. If the weather is fine they have a chance to let off steam playing football and throwing balls about on the beautiful meadow around the Cathedral, before getting down to the serious business!

Holding their attention and commitment is all-important. Awards are made at year-end for attendance, and choristers vote for the one among them who has been most inspiring. 'They feel that they're doing something which is important and are part of a family. They also become more interested in Christianity and worship. Its like the pebble in a pool – the implications reach out'.

Brecon Cathedral Organ

It appears that a main organ at the priory church came from the Drury Lane Theatre London in 1789 and was probably built by Henry Holland in 1787. It was replaced by a new one in 1886 built by William Hill and Son at a net cost of £1,100. David Gedge surmises that the Drury Lane organ found a new home at Clydach in the Swansea Valley.

Thomas Hill, elder son of the original William Hill, was in charge of the firm and as could be expected of a company who supervised the building or restoration of such famous organs as those at Beverley Minster; Kings College, Cambridge; Ely and Litchfield, the one at Brecon was a tonal success. But in other ways namely, that because the organ chamber was sited in a small, low-roofed chapel opening out of the South Transept, the organist accompanying the choir experienced considerable difficulty in hearing the singing. It was in 1927, the organ now 41 years old and in need of restoration, that the difficulty was partially resolved by removing it into a specially built chamber above the former one. The final resolution which permitted the organ tones to permeate fully into the building was achieved in 1931. It was now possible for organist Humphrey Carden to establish a tradition of organ recitals in the Cathedral: he began with renowned Birmingham Town Hall Organist George Cunningham giving a recital on the rebuilt instrument. Others were to follow, Percy Hall of Hereford Cathedral and George Thalben Ball (successor to Walford Davies at the Temple Church, London). The recitals continued even during the Second World War with events by Harry Goss-Custard, the Liverpool Cathedral Organist and concerts by the Brecon Cathedral Choir and the Breconshire Orchestral Society, conducted by Humphrey Carden.

Further work on the organ in 1962 was to improve clarity for both organist and singers but organist Gwerfyl Davies did not have much time to enjoy that luxury because later in the year he moved from Brecon to become Music Adviser to the City of Leicester. That enjoyable experience was to befall his successor M. Bryan Hesford who was Organist and Choirmaster of Wymondham Abbey in Norfolk before coming to Brecon.

David Gedge and his wife Hazel Davies commenced duties in 1966. In August 1972, smoke was seen emitting from the main Cathedral Organ. As it happens it was caused by only a minor electrical fault, but it signalled the urgent need for a major overhaul. With the 50th anniversary of the Diocese imminent in 1973 and celebratory plans by Bishop J.J.A. Thomas were well in hand, there was no time to lose. The estimated cost for rebuilding and tonal remodelling of the organ by Percy Daniel was £11,580. The Bishop – a keen musician –

immediately set about raising the money as one of the acts of thanksgiving to commemorate the Jubilee. The opportunity was taken to re-model the instrument, placing the newly-created Positive Organ in the space previously occupied by the console and great care taken to preserve the unique William Hill tonal quality. The work was completed in time for Easter Day, April 22nd 1973, when the Archbishop of Wales preached at Choral Eucharist. The redesigned organ was voted a great success, a triumphant achievement betwixt the Cathedral Organist David Gedge and Walter Gulvin of Percy Daniel and Co. along with many helpful suggestions from Kelvin Redford of the local Christ College and Hazel Davies who acted as Assistant Organists.

The 1995 rebuild, also by Percy Daniel and Co. Ltd., completed the scheme started in 1973.

In 2006, six new digital stops were added by Phoenix Organs.

Potted Profile

Musical Director and Organist: Mark Duthie. Appointed 2007. Born in Aberdeen.
Appointments: Assistant Organist Chester Cathedral followed by Assistant Master of Music at Peterborough Cathedral (13 years) where he also ran a Girls Choir. Appointed to Brecon Cathedral 2007.
Assistant Organist: Meirion Wyn Jones. Appointed 2007. Born Llangollen 1972. Educated: Ysgol Dinas

Brân. Wells Cathedral School, Somerset. Course in Organ Playing (5 years). Then Organ Scholar at Winchester Cathedral (12 months). Scholarship to Royal Academy of Music and Organ Scholar at Westminster Abbey and organist at Ealing Place Holborn.

Appointments: Organist Liverpool R.C. Cathedral. Organist at The Oratory Edgebaston. Organist at Abergavenny Parish Church. Assistant Organist Brecon Cathedral working alongside Mark Duthie 2007.

Meirion Wyn Jones BMus; ARCO is a composer, singer (tenor) and Official Accompanist to both the Llangollen International Eisteddfod and the National Eisteddfod of Wales.

Meirion Wyn Jones relinquished his position in December 2011 to pursue his freelance engagements. His role at Brecon has been taken by Paul Hayward, (formerly of Nottingham Cathedral), in a position now twinned with the post of Organist in Residence at Christ College Brecon.

Adventures of an Organ from Hay Castle

Possibly the most exiting venture during David Gedge's period as cathedral organist was the restoration of the old chamber organ standing in the South Transept. The Dean and Chapter had decided to sell the instrument as scrap. Fortunately at the insistence of Mr Gedge, Dean Ungoed Jacob persuaded the Chapter to suspend this decision pending an enquiry into the state of the pipework by London Organist Robert Munns. In the course of preparing a report on the organ, certain facts came to light which excited Robert Munns and delighted David Gedge. If only organs could speak, this one certainly had a very interesting story to tell! It was known that it had come from Hay Castle, Hay on Wye, some twenty miles away, and referred to in the famous Kilvert Diaries (March 3rd 1870 and May 7th 1872). Built at Greek Street, Soho in London by Henry Bevington and Sons in 1789 and possibly rebuilt fifty years later, it remained at Hay Castle until the Vicar of Hay, Archdeacon W.L. Bevan retired from the Castle in 1901. The Vicar then moved to Ely Tower, Brecon, the organ then presumably being placed in store. Certainly after 1907 it was moved to Pool House, Belmont Road, Hereford the home of Mrs Mumford, grand-daughter of Archdeacon Bevan. Here it stood in the hall until 1923, when Mrs Mumford moved to Weymouth.

This was the year when Edward Latham Bevan, son of Archdeacon Bevan, Teddy Bevan of the Kilvert Diaries, became the first Bishop of the newly formed Diocese of Swansea and Brecon. It was he who brought the organ to the Chapel of the Guild of Cordwainers in the Cathedral. There it remained until 1963 when it was moved to allow for the completion of the screen around this chapel, but in doing so some of the pipework was damaged. An estimate of £800 for its complete restoration by Percy Daniel and Co. Ltd, Organ Builders of Clevedon, Avon was actioned, financed thanks to the Kilvert Society, Friends of Brecon Cathedral and private donations. The organ came back from Avon fully restored, and mounted on a platform on wheels with an electric blower so that it could be used anywhere in the Cathedral, but otherwise left in its original condition, with some of its quirkier characteristics retained! On the following April 1st 1972 – Holy Saturday – the chamber organ was given a good workout in a performance of J.S. Bach's St John Passion. Shortly afterwards, Hazel Davies recorded the 'Twelve Short Pieces' (composed by Samuel Wesley for such an organ) for BBC Radio 3. David Gedge's insistence on the organ's restoration was fully vindicated!

Bishops

1923-34	Edward Latham Bevan – Teddy Bevan of the Kilvert Diaries – ref Kilvert Diary Wednesday February 7, 1872 – (formerly Assistant Bishop of Swansea Diocese of St Davids)
1934-39	John Morgan
1939-53	Edward William Williamson
1953-58	William Glyn Hughes Simon
1958-76	John James Absalom Thomas
1976-88	Benjamin Noel Young Vaughan
1988-99	Dewi Morris Bridges
1999-2008	Anthony Edward Pierce
2008-	John David Edward Davies

St David's Cathedral – Eglwys Gadeiriol Tyddewi

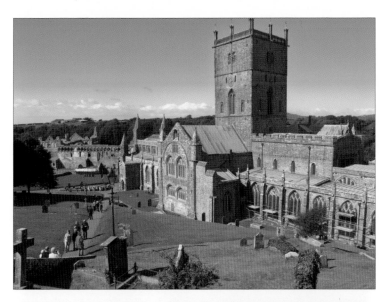

Llandaff Cathedral

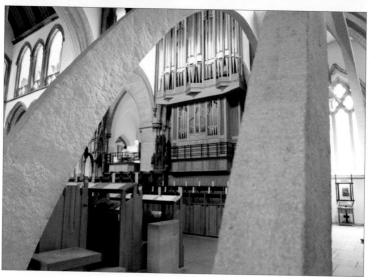

Brecon Cathedral

St Asaph Cathedral

St Woolos' Cathedral, Newport, Diocese of Monmouth

Bangor Cathedral

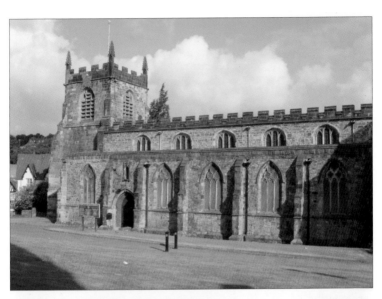

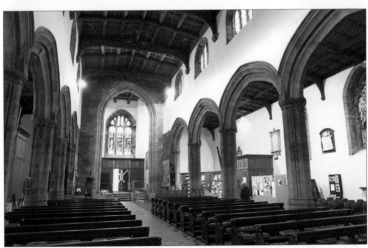

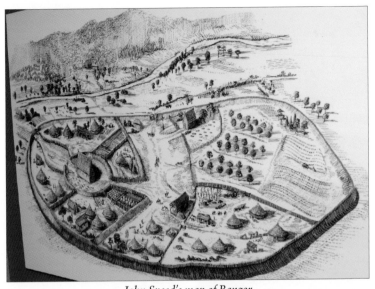

John Speed's map of Bangor

Deans

1939-49	Edward Albert Trevillian Roberts
1949-64	William Edward Jones
1964-67	John Gwynno James
1967-78	William Ungoed Jacob
1979-82	Alwyn Rice Jones
1982-93	David Huw Jones
1993-98	John Harris
1998-2000	Geraint Morgan Hugh Hughes
2000-2008	John David Edward Davies
2008-	Geoffrey Osborne Marshall

Organists

1879-1918	Rees Thomas Heins
1918-23	Ernest William Baker
1923-56	John Humphrey Carden
1956-62	David Gwerfyl Davies
1963-66	Michael Bryan Hesford
1966-2007	David Patrick Gedge
2007-	Mark Duthie

The Bishop

The Rt Revd John David Edward Davies, born 1953, has been Bishop of Swansea and Brecon since 2008 and lists among his recreations: music, especially opera, organ and 60s and 70s pop. His career has progressed from articled clerk in 1975 to a solicitor from 1977 to 1982; then becoming assistant curate at Chepstow from 1984 to 1986, curate in charge at Michaelstone-y-Fedw with Rudry 1986 to 1988, succeeded by becoming Rector of Bedwas with Rudry from 1988 to 1995, Newport (Maindee) 1995 to 2000, then Dean of Brecon from 2000 to 2008 and his enthronement at Brecon in that year.

The Dean

The Very Revd Geoffrey Osborne Marshall, a native of Rossett in North Wales (b. 1948), was appointed Dean of Brecon in 2008, and lists leading pilgrimages to the Middle East and walking among his recreational activities.

He began his professional career as a curate in Waltham Cross (1973-76), followed by Digswell Welwyn Garden City (1976-78); priest in Christ Church Belper (1978-86), vicar of Spondon Derby (1986-93), canon missioner Derby Cathedral (1993-2002) director of ordinands (1995-2000), Rector and Area Dean of Wrexham 2002-08, before becoming the Dean at Brecon and Warden of Readers for the Diocese.

He was Chaplain of Derby HS (1987-2001), Rural Dean Derby North (1990-95), Canon of St Asaph Cathedral (2004). In 1984 he received the St Martin's Religious Broadcasting Award while at BBC Radio Derby. He is a director of Shelter Cymru, Brecon Beacons Tourism, Churches Tourism Association, McCabe Educational Trust and several local charities.

The Cathedral Church of St John The Evangelist Brecon

Bishop: John David Edward Davies
Dean: Geoffrey Osborne Marshall
Director of Music: Mark Duthie
Organist: Paul Hayward
The Cathedral Office: Cathedral Close, Brecon LD3 9DP.
Telephone: 01874 623 857
email: admin@breconcathedral.org.uk
Cathedral website: www.breconcathedral.org.uk

Sunday Services

8.00 am	Said Eucharist
11.00 am	Sung Eucharist
(3rd Sunday – Matins)	
3.30 pm	Choral Evensong

Weekday Services

Daily:

8.30 am	Morning Prayer
5.45 pm	Evening Prayer (Except Saturday)
Friday:	5.45 Choral Evensong
Monday:	09.00 am (Said Eucharist)
Tuesday:	09.00 am

Wednesday:	11.00 am
Thursday:	09.00 am
Friday:	12.00 noon
Saturday:	09.00 am

Monthly Service

Healing Eucharist: 12 noon first Thursday in every month.

Sources

The Cathedral Church of St John The Evangelist Brecon, published by the 'Friends of Brecon Cathedral' (1994).

Rod Cooper, *Abbeys and Priories of Wales,* published by Christopher Davies Ltd Swansea (1993).

Brecon Cathedral – A Guide to 'The Cathedral Church of St John the Evangelist Brecon'.

David Gedge, *A Country Cathedral Organist Looks Back* (2005) and *More from a Country Cathedral Organist* (2008)', published by Serendipity, Darlington.

Enid Bird, *The Organists and Organs of the Welsh Cathedrals in the 20th Century*, published by Enid Bird, 16 Miller Ave, Wakefield, West Yorkshire, WF2 7DJ. Phone 01924 250 115.

Kilvert's Diary 1870-1879, An Illustrated Selection Edited and Introduced by William Plomer, published by David R. Godine, Boston, Mass U.S.A. 1986.

David Hugh Farmer, *The Oxford Dictionary of Saints,* published by Oxford University Press 1992.

Brecon Cathedral website.

Beacon – The Church Magazine for Brecon Cathedral.

Tim McCormick, *The Cathedrals, Abbeys & Priories of Wales,* published by Logaston Press 2010.

Very Reverend Geoffrey Osborne Marshall – Dean of Brecon Cathedral. (interview).

Lieut Col Rodney Ashwood – Cathedral warden. (interview).

Merial Rice Jones (widow of Alwyn Rice Jones, Dean of Brecon 1979-82, then Bishop of St Asaph and later Archbishop of Wales). (interview).

Mark Duthie – Musical Director Brecon Cathedral (interview).

Meirion Wyn Jones – Organist Brecon Cathedral up to December 2011. (interview).

Llandaff Cathedral

[the cathedral church of ss peter and paul with
ss dyfrig, teilo and euddogwy]

*So much to see, so many questions to ask! Llandaff
Cathedral is a rare combination of the very ancient
and the ultra new, so often it has faced destruction by
various agencies, each time it has renewed itself!
Much of what you see is relatively new,
but in character, thanks to skilful craftsmen,
it's a medieval Cathedral rooted in a
Celtic tradition.*

A quarter hour bus ride out of the centre of Cardiff gets you to the 'village' of Llandaff, population 9,000. It's an incredible journey, it might as well be a million miles away from the bustling capital of Wales, such is the contrast. And down in the wooded ravine, the site of Llandaff Cathedral, birdsong abounds. At the top of the escarpment, there's a playful duel between a crow and a grey squirrel disputing the contents of a bin they've raided!

Here then is the unlikely location of Llandaff Cathedral, where Archbishop of Wales Barry Morgan is also the Diocesan Bishop in the country's most populist diocese. It was here in the Age of the Saints circa 560, that the Welsh saints, set up a Christian community.

Cathedral Archivist John Bethell reasons that 'There's been a Christian community here at least since the year 500 and possibly a hundred years before that.

There's a theory that a site like this was chosen because it was out of sight of pirates on the River Taff, where there was quite a lot of unlawful behaviour going on.

And there was another reason, the major east west route went along the eastern end of the cathedral. At that time the river ran just beyond the trees, where it could be crossed. It was a natural site for a little village or hamlet, ideally suited to locate a monastic community'.

'Its hard for us now to appreciate the strength of the Celtic Church in the 5th and 6th centuries', says John Bethell. 'They had a base here as well as at Llandeilo and at Llantwitmajor, some 20 miles away down on the coast. But they were not monasteries similar to the Medieval ones, rather they were communities of Christians who had a fairly good understanding and standard of education. It's difficult to imagine that level of sophistication alongside the general social conditions of the time'. At the same time he concedes the paucity of tangible evidence from those days. So when the Welsh Bishop Urban (Welsh: Gwrgan), a Norman appointee of clerical stock, came along in 1107 with the wherewithal to build his first major cathedral, albeit half the size of the present structure, there was already a well established Christian tradition here'.

Nick Lambert asserts that 'Christianity came to South Wales around the third century when the Roman converts Julius and Aaron were martyred at Caerleon in 304 AD, leaving behind a saintly cult that persisted through to the Middle Ages'.

It is a place where Teilo's spiritual legacy holds true, and his mortal remains are entombed. Further it is said

Urban, brought Dyfrig's remains here to Llandaff from Bardsey, island of the Saints, in 1120.

Parts of Bishop Urban's Norman Cathedral remain, the arch at the west front main entrance is one fine example, which dates from 1170 when the building was enlarged. To the left of the doorway is the Jasper Tower (1485) the gift of Jasper Tudor, Lord of Glamorgan (uncle of Henry VII) which houses a ring of thirteen bells. The perpendicular parapet on top embellished with nicely done tracery is a later 19th century refinement. The west wall dates from the 12th century while the tower and spire are a Victorian restoration of late 15th century twin towers which crashed in a great storm in 1722.

Saint Teilo's memory is cherished at Llandaff. Mr Bethell relates a tale which underlines this strong attachment. 'We had an extremely wealthy family living in the area in the middle ages named Mathews who had right to burial in the north aisle of the cathedral', he says. 'In return they were required to maintain the north aisle. For some unclear reason they left the area in about 1600 and their association with the cathedral came to an end. But we still have 3 tombs of the family who were buried here.

We had a very interesting letter in the early 1990s, addressed to the Dean, from a member of the Mathews family living in Australia. The letter said that they had the skull of St Teilo and wondered whether we'd like to have it in Llandaff cathedral. "It's in the vault of an Australian bank at the moment", they said.

It was a huge dilemma, the Anglican church doesn't venerate relics as the medieval church did, we don't do anything with relics in the Anglican church now. But for the sake of history and its important link with Llandaff we took it, and it's now kept in a locked cupboard in the St Teilo chapel and brought out for display annually on February 9th, his Feast Day. The Dean didn't send it for carbon dating to test its authenticity – the dean of St David's experience with "David's" bones must have sent foreboding signals! We have many visitors to the cathedral who are members of the Mathews family from all over the world. They disappeared from active service here in 1630'. Beautifully encrusted in silver the skull may have been used as a drinking cup from a holy well, a christening vessel or in a sacrament service. It's now appropriately held safely in the St Teilo Chapel since 1994, a location created by architect Donald Buttress.

But the Cathedral's very existence today is either a stroke of luck or sheer fate, because in 1941 (2nd January) a wartime German Landmine parachute snagged on the Cathedral's spire, which resulted in the bomb being flung into the cemetery a matter of but a few yards from the main building, with a thunderous explosion. It caused a huge crater when a vast amount of earth was thrown up, gravestones hurled, one fully 150 yards away up on to the village green. Most of the Cathedral's main roof crashed in, internal furnishings including the pulpit were damaged beyond repair, stonework was badly impaired. It was a scene of gross devastation, the Cathedral's darkest hour. Precious stained glass was shattered, save for twelve windows which had previously been removed for safe keeping.

Remarkably the low pitched Lady Chapel roof was intact and part of the roof over the High Altar was not destroyed, these were sections of the Cathedral which were soon brought back into use again.

Built in c1280 the Lady Chapel, possibly the oldest part of the cathedral, had remained largely unaltered, save for decoration, since it was first built. ('One of the glories of the Cathedral now' is the very striking Jesse Window (Isaiah X1:1) there, by Geoffrey Webb, a 1951 replacement of the Thomas Willement armorial glass lost in the bombing).

But it took 16 years before the Cathedral could be fully used once more. An obelisk is all that now marks the spot where the bomb dropped – a symbol of peaceful tranquillity.

That this Cathedral has survived at all is a wonder, given that during its long history for several hundreds of years, up to the 19th century, it was in a state of dereliction. At the time of the Reformation the silver shrine of St Teilo was broken, valuables, vestments and money were taken away. About a hundred years later, in 1646, Cromwell's troops in the Civil War turned the Cathedral nave into 'an ale house, the choir became a calf pen, one part of the building was used as a stable ... the font became a hog trough'. A storm in 1703 brought the Jasper Tower pinnacles crashing through the roof; in 1722 the damage was compounded when the south-west tower collapsed in a storm and the roof of the nave fell in. Decay and storm damage took its toll, the cathedral's condition was akin to the ruins of Tintern or Valle Crucis' Abbey. So really it was in the condition in which you now see ruined abbeys.

At that time of decay, architect John Wood of Bath was appointed in 1736 to see what he could make of it. Given that there weren't sufficient funds to restore all the nave, what he created was a rather unusual Georgian building known as the 'Italian Temple' which occupied the space between the choir and the Lady Chapel. It was a strange structure with a little low pedimented west front actually sitting in amongst the ruin.

That served for about 100 years, but towards the middle of the 19th century there became a great arousal of interest in church building far and wide. Also a huge upsurge in prosperity in this part of the country, due to the rise of a vibrant iron and coal industry. This of course generated the creation of docks along the coast in Newport, Cardiff, Barry and Swansea together with an enormous amount of wealth. Bishop Alfred Ollivant, the Manchester born Welsh speaking bishop here from 1849 to 1882, proved to be a sort of catalyst for this prosperity, rapidly raising huge sums of money, so that piece by piece, by 1869 the ruin was transformed: within thirty years the Cathedral had been restored!

The architects were Pritchard & Seddon. The commission had been given to John Pritchard, a young architect just making his way, who then formed an alliance with the well established J. F. Seddon, a Londoner. As you go into the Cathedral today you will see much of their influence still in evidence, how they were able to retain its medieval character, and introduce much of the Pre-Raphaelite movement's work into stained glass and art works. Artwork by Rossetti, Burne-Jones, Ford Madox Brown and William Morris abound. This came about says John Bethell through the good offices of Seddon's brother, who was himself a member of the Arts and Crafts Movement. 'Inspired by William Morris, the Movement had their "stained glass workshop" producing windows to order; panels could be acquired ready-made from a catalogue'.

The most surprising thing of all is that the Cathedral still exists after the 1941 bomb blast. It is largely due to the vision of architect George Pace (1915-1975) with his sympathetic understanding of church restoration, and a feel for the Arts and Crafts movement, that the restoration was achieved. He was the one entrusted with the mammoth task.

Matching the stonework itself was challenging – the Cathedral contains a variety of stone in its construction, some limestone from Cowbridge, several different kinds of yellowy stone from Somerset and the Cotswolds, and some of the poorer reddish stone which was quarried two miles up the road at Radyr. 'It's a huge study in itself' says Mr Bethell. The construction work on the Cathedral fabric tested Pace's innate skill, as was making good the top of the spire made unsafe when the landmine parachute snagged on it. Likewise the internal furnishings had to be remade to tone in with the Cathedral's medieval character.

What people now tend to remember most about Llandaff is the Majestas – Christ in Majesty, Jacob

Epstein's masterpiece. 'It was very controversial when it first went up, it still draws strong reactions!', says Mr Bethell. 'We've got used to it, we like it. What concerns many people is the insertion of a very modern concrete arch into a medieval building. In the middle of the 20th century it was popular imagery, we're looking at it 50 years on'.

One of the things that prompted it was that this cathedral lacked a division between the nave and the more sacred area, the chancel and the sanctuary and so on, and even before the war they were looking for a solution to this. Pace conceived this to give some division yet not to interrupt the vista; his intention was to create a series of inter connected spaces to give the sense of a much greater length than it really is. You can now see the window in the 'far distance': that was intentional. The pulpit designed by George Pace, replaced the very ornate Victorian pulpit by Pritchard & Seddon which could not be repaired because of bomb damage, so he produced a black pulpit. Finely adorned with a curious collection of fairly traditional decoration, it is a strange departure from his usual work, which is easily identified by his liking for light oak furniture, which is limed and goes darker as time goes on.

George Pace's skill is further exemplified in the regimental chapel known as St David Chapel which was built in 1957. During the war the Welsh regiment had the idea that when peace was restored they'd like to have a chapel commemorating the fallen, so this was built as part of the post war restoration. It's entirely modern in concept, even down to the frontal and altar furniture. It's a very fine addition to the cathedral and well used by the Regiment as well as for Eucharist and cathedral services. Located in what was formerly part of the church yard, Pace's idea was to incorporate the chapel so as to amalgamate it with the processional route connecting the cathedral with the Prebendal House which accommodates the clergy robing rooms. The processional corridor enters the cathedral through an archway which was formerly a main cathedral outer entrance dating to Bishop Urban's time and is known as Porth Teilo (Teilo's Doorway). This leads into the north aisle and up to the high altar, a very practical sort of arrangement.

The whole idea was begun during the war with a service in the roofless nave to launch a building fund: the cathedral architect at that time being the eminent Sir Charles Nicholson, he quite quickly produced his own Gothic plan.

When Pace took over on the demise of Sir Charles Nicholson in 1949, those plans were set to one side in favour of his own design.

The various campaigns the regiment was involved in, and how it has evolved in more recent times after several amalgamations into the Royal Regiment of Wales, are commemorated. All this mirrors the Regimental Chapel in Brecon Cathedral where the Regiment have a strong military base.

A buttress which was once on the 'outside' of the cathedral remains near the archway. 'This Norman "external doorway" dates back to the first part of this current building with probably a small timber porch, because this was once the main entrance to the cathedral' says Mr Bethell.

Nearby there's an ancient effigy which once stood on a ledge at the apex above the present entrance to the cathedral. For many centuries, possibly since the 13th century, it had stood in its niche on the west wall. 'But it was cleaned in 1984 and brought inside for preservation from further weather erosion'. Believed to be the original medieval Majestas, Christ in Majesty, on account of the halo, it had been there free standing in its niche, impervious to lasting damage by storm or even the blast of Hitler's bomb!

Due left of the main entrance there is a tiny chapel dedicated to St Illtud. Here on the north wall there is a triptych by Dante Gabriel Rossetti. Originally the three panels were placed behind the High Altar during the Victorian restoration. It was removed for safety before the Cathedral was bombed.

For some time after the war there had been dissatisfaction with the high altar arrangement, Pace following an earlier suggestion, took the whole lot away and created the little St Illtud chapel, and made the triptych a centrepiece, which works very well. It's a painting which at the time of the restoration was recognised as a fine Victorian painting, but it's only in recent times that everyone has realised that pre-Raphaelite paintings are extremely valuable. 'So we're a little nervous about it, hence the metal gates and the decoration by architect Donald Buttress (who followed after Pace's days), which present it in a better way, and give it some kind of security'. The centrepiece is the Nativity, the figure on the left is David as a boy complete with his sling, and on the right as king. The creation of this chapel and restoration of the Jasper Tower, part of the postwar restoration,was financed by the 53rd Welsh (Infantry) Division plus a vast amount of money from s'Hertogenbosch a town in Holland (in appreciation of the 53rd Welsh (Infantry) Division who liberated the town after a 3 day siege). So in gratitude they put in a lot of money to create this chapel. And they presented a roll of honour for this Regiment – it's a nice connection that has been maintained.'

During all the rebuilding it appears that at least St Teilo's Tomb has remained constant, positioned as it is on the south wall of the presbytery next to the altar. 'This was a creation in the 19th century restoration, a best estimate of what it was like' says Mr Bethell, 'the little scenes below are from the life of Teilo, an acknowledged leader of the early church. The beautiful original Tomb with precious stones was whisked away at the time of the Reformation – to save it from removal by the iconoclasts'.

Mr Bethell believes that the mortal remains of other Saints could well be here under the Cathedral or its surrounding area. 'Some of the vast number buried in the cathedral grounds are unmarked, and could date back to the cathedral's earliest times. The Burial Register only starts in 1724', he explains.

Among those buried in the vaults, now filled in, under the Cathedral, is Benjamin Hall, 1st Baron Llanover PC

(1802-1867), who was Commissioner of Works when the Houses of Parliament were built, and is generally believed to have been immortalized by having Big Ben named in his honour!

Music at Llandaff

It appears that the history of music at Llandaff has been uneven. For long periods the Cathedral's fabric and establishment was in decline. In 1691 we learn how the choir was suppressed, the organ destroyed, and the national schoolmaster appointed to lead the singing for £4 a year!

Even at Bishop Alfred Olivant's enthronement in March 1850, these pathetic arrangements were still the rule, for we read that 'On the opening of the door to the bishop's summons ... the national schoolmaster, heading the procession, gave out a Psalm, which was sung by a dozen of his scholars, a bass viol being the only instrument then in the possession of the Cathedral. In this way the bishop was conducted to his throne'. (Bishop's Charge).

But under the rule of this enlightened bishop we see many changes in the fortunes of the Cathedral, some of which, such as rescuing the building from a near ruin has been referred to already. During this time of restoration in 1861 an organ by Gray and Davison was installed and the Choral Service, which had been discontinued since 1691, revived. Dean Vaughan, a former Headmaster of Harrow, installed at Llandaff in 1879, aware of the musical shortcomings, established the Cathedral Choir School in the old Deanery, a house on the green, in 1880.

In October 1958 the Choir School relocated to the Georgian building, which had once been the Bishop's Palace. This is now an independent fee-paying non-residential institution, part of the Woodard Corporation, providing education of a very high order for 650 children with an age ranging from 3 to 16 years. Membership of the Cathedral Choir is conditional on children receiving their education at the Choir School. Bursaries are awarded annually for suitable children, who from about 8 years old having had a successful interview and voice test with the Musical Director Richard Moorhouse, will for a year become probationary choristers. This is important because it will show whether they fit in to a very demanding life. It's a commitment not to be taken lightly, by the children or their parents. At the school the choristers are given a sound general education plus further musical instruction and the opportunity for training to play the piano, or a string or a brass instrument.

Musically it's a first class education (led by Head of the Musical Department) which often leads them on to related careers: a former chorister went on to a senior position in the Musical Department at Harvard University in America.

School day normally begins in the Cathedral at 8 o'clock with a rehearsal taken by the Musical Director, before going over to the school by 9 for their lessons. After school, at 5 o'clock, there will be another rehearsal for evensong. Mondays are for girls, who are joined by the 'Consort', a group of people who enjoy singing, and they also sing evensong on Wednesdays. The choir boys sing evensong on Tuesdays and Fridays. The lay clerks, 12 in number, comprising mainly of students at the Welsh College of Music and Drama, and at the Cardiff University working or studying, sing the Thursday evensong. The men and boys together sing the Saturday evensong. Then on Sunday they come to the Cathedral at 10 o'clock to rehearse for the 11 o'clock service which finishes at 12. They then come back for a 2.30 rehearsal for the 3.30 evensong.

Sunday at Llandaff is a supremely uplifting musical and spiritual experience. As the Reverend Canon Graham Holcombe, a moving spirit in the Cathedral's musical life explains: The Cathedral is also the parish church of Llandaff, so Sunday services start with Matins at 7.30 am, sometimes followed by Litany in Lent and Advent. Then at 8 there's a said Eucharist in the nave, and at 9 o'clock a parish Eucharist with the parish choir consisting of boys, girls and adults. The Cathedral Choir sing in the 11 o'clock service; at 12.30 there's the Said Eucharist; and they sing again at 3.30 for the fully choral evensong. And then at 5.30 the Parish Choir (the adults without the children) sing compline. Music is an offering which goes back to monastic days, people often don't sing the psalms at Evensong – the Choir do it on their behalf as an offering of musical excellence in the worship of God.

There's also the Llandaff Cathedral Choral Society which meet every Monday. They perform oratorios and do two concerts every year. It began as a voluntary choir who sang when the Cathedral Choir was on holiday.

Apart from the Parish Choir in the care of parish

organist David Thomas, there's also the 'Merbecke Choir' which any member of the Cathedral congregation can join. Its conductor is Dr Poole, a lay clerk, and the organist is Canon Graham Holcombe. They too are available to be drafted in to sing in the Cathedral services.

At the time of writing this book (2012) Llandaff Festival, established in 2008, was still in a state of euphoria following the installation of their new Nicholson Organ during Easter 2010. The Festival in partnership with the Royal College of Music and Drama is not only a celebration of this event and an opportunity for exceptionally talented musicians to perform in the exquisite acoustics of Llandaff Cathedral, but also a money raising event to meet the remaining cost of 'its Solo and completed Pedal organ'. Festival Director Canon Graham Holcombe, a native of Port Talbot who has had a long association with Llandaff Cathedral and was for 17 years vicar of four churches in neighbouring Pentyrch, a very accomplished organist, is full of enthusiasm for the organ. He says 'The Llandaff organ can be regarded as the largest completed British organ since the one at Coventry Cathedral in 1958, a very fine musical instrument for Llandaff Cathedral where musical excellence is given a high priority in its worship'.

In giving a resumé of events leading to this development Richard Moorhouse, Musical Director since 2000, a graduate of the Royal Academy of Music and Organ Scholar at Westminster Abbey, then Assistant Sub-Organist at St Paul's Cathedral says: 'For over thirty years, discussions had taken place concerning the Cathedral's organ. Re-built after the Cathedral was bomb damaged in 1941, it was very much an instrument subjected to the restraints of that time. It was poorly located, with a cramped internal lay out and surrounded by screens which prevented the sound from being effective in the building.

For decades its general condition had been in decline, making it unreliable and very expensive to repair: a lightning strike in February 2007 finally rendered it unusable for the daily services. This is what led to the decision to replace the organ with a completely new instrument. After much deliberation, the plans put forward by Nicholsons of Malvern were chosen. Their proposal was for the largest, wholly new, British built organ to be commissioned in a UK cathedral for nearly half a century. It would be built in two symmetrical cases situated either side of the choir stalls and contain a total of 4870 pipes, varying in size from those the size of a pencil to ones 32 ft in length and big enough for a person to fit inside: the 77 speaking stops being divided across four manuals and pedals.

Work at the factory began in the middle of 2008, moving to the cathedral in April 2009. After 30,000 man hours work it was done: our Cathedral, a beautiful and historic building, had gained a new dimension! The magnificent new organ-cases frame Sir Jacob Epstein's statue of Christ in Majesty, the unique architectural feature which is recognised all over the World.

The organ accompanies the Choir and therefore needs to have the tonal variety and subtlety necessary for this purpose. It is also essential that it can lead large congregations in the singing of hymns, as well as being flexible to allow the playing of a world wide organ repertoire. Those of us who have had the privilege of hearing and playing the new instrument have been stunned by the quality of the sounds it creates. These range from the beauty of a single, quiet flute, to the majestic sound of full organ. Llandaff Cathedral now has an organ that will re-enforce its place on the international map of musical excellence. The Cathedral is not only a place of worship, it's also a venue for concerts, recordings and broadcasts. At a cost of £1.5m it represents a great act of faith and has already created world wide interest, and praise at the highest level from a number of eminent organists'.

Archbishop Barry Morgan, a native of Gwaun-Cae-Gurwen near Neath in South Wales has been Bishop of Llandaff since 1999 and Archbishop of Wales since 2003 having previously served as Bishop of Bangor from 1993 to 1999. His education took in history at London, Theology at Cambridge and he trained for the Ministry at Westcott House, Cambridge. He studied for a doctorate whilst a university lecturer. Barry Morgan has worked in a range of ministerial contexts including parish ministry, university and theological college lecturer, university chaplain, archdeacon, director of ordinands and as a continuing ministerial education officer. He has served on the Central Committee of the World Council of Churches, served on the Primates Standing Committee of the Anglican Communion and was a member of the Lambeth Commission which produced the Windsor Report in 2004. He has published a number of articles and books including a study of the work of the Welsh poet R. S. Thomas, 'Strangely Orthodox'. Currently Pro-Chancellor of the University of Wales, a fellow of Cardiff, UWIC, Bangor, Carmarthen, Swansea and Lampeter. He was President of the Welsh Centre for International Affairs for six years, he has chaired an inquiry on behalf of Shelter Cymru into homelessness in Wales. Recreationally he enjoys reading novels and playing golf.

Assistant Bishop David Wilbourne was born in Derbyshire (1955), educated in Yorkshire, and then went on to Jesus College and Westcott House, Cambridge where he studied Natural Sciences and Theology. Then for six years, prior to his ordination, he worked for Barclays Bank. His calling into the priesthood began in Middlesborough, followed by a move as rector to a semi-rural parish north of Pontefract. Here he ran a class on Ancient Greek for twenty parishioners. Next, in 1991, he transferred to Bishopthorpe and became chaplain to the Archbishop of York, John Habgood. Four years later, upon his retirement, David Wilbourne continued the work with his successor, David Hope. Here he was also Director of Ordinands, selecting men and women for the ordained ministry and taking them through training to their first post. In 1997 he was moved to be Vicar of Helmsley, a moorland market town in North Yorkshire were he became chairman of the governors of the high achieving Ryedale Comprehensive. In 2008 Archbishop Sentamu made him a canon of York, and in April 2009 he was consecrated Assistant Bishop of Llandaff.

David Wilbourne, has a fair amount of ink coursing his veins: his first book, 'An Archbishop's Diary' was published in 1995, followed by 'A Vicar's Diary' and 'A Summer's Diary' – books which are being sold by the Cathedral in aid of the Organ Fund. His other books are 'A Virgin's Diary' and 'You were made for me' and currently he's working on the authorised biography of John Habgood. Prior to coming to Wales he was for twelve years a regular Church Times diarist. A Society of Authors Member, he's also a popular after-dinner speaker, broadcaster, retreat and conference leader.

Dean John Lewis (retired 2012) was ordained a deacon in 1973 and priest in 1974, then served as a curate in Whitchurch followed by Lisvane, before becoming chaplain at Cardiff University (1980-1985). Appointed vicar of St David's Brecon (with Llanspyddid and Llanilltyd) in 1985, next moving to Bassaleg in 1991, he became Dean of Llandaff in 2000. Additional to his parish duties he has served as secretary of the Provincial Selection Panel of the Church in Wales and as chaplain for Continuing Ministerial Education for the Bishop of Monmouth.

Born in 1947 John Lewis was educated at Dyffryn Grammar School before winning a scholarship to Jesus College Oxford where he studied mathematics. Upon obtaining his BA degree in 1969 and a diploma in applied statistics the following year, he went on to St John's College, Cambridge where he studied theology in preparation for his ordination into the ministry.

Llandaff Cathedral

Bishop: The Most Reverend Dr Barry Morgan, Archbishop of Wales and Bishop of Llandaff.

Assistant Bishop: The Right Reverend David Wilbourne.

Dean: The Very Reverend John Lewis (retired 2012).

Organist and Master of the Choristers: Richard Moorhouse, GRSM, LRAM, ARCM.

Assistant Organist: Sachin Y C S Gunga.

Second Assistant Organist & Director of the Parish Choir: David Thomas, MA, B.Mus, ARCO, ARCM.

Director of the Cathedral Girls' Choir: Simon Lovell-Jones, BA.

Assistant Organist to the Girls' Choir: James Bull, B.Mus.

Conductor Cathedral Choral Society: Dominic Neville, MA, (Cantab), PGCE.

Director of Llandaff Festival: Reverend Canon Graham Holcombe, BA,FRSA.

Administration: Cathedral Office, Administration Office, Prebendal House, Llandaff, Cardiff CF5 2LA. Tel: (029) 2056 4554.

E-mail: office@llandaffcathedral.org.uk

Website: www.churchinwales.org.uk

Cathedral Administrator: Michael Turk.

Office Assistant: Annette Parkes.

Times of Services

Sundays

7.30 am	Matins (Said)
8.00 am	Holy Eucharist
9.00 am	Parish Eucharist
11.00 am	Choral Eucharist
12.30 pm	Holy Eucharist (Lady Chapel)
3.30 pm	Choral Evensong
5.30 pm	Compline (Lady Chapel)

Daily Services

Monday

9.30 am	Holy Eucharist (St Dyfrig Chapel)
5.30 pm	Evensong

Tuesday

9.30 am	Yr Offeren (St Dyfrig Chapel)
6.00 pm	Evensong

Wednesday

9.30 am	Holy Eucharist (St David Chapel)
5.30 pm	Evensong
7.00 pm	Holy Eucharist (St Dyfrig Chapel)

Thursday

10.00 am	Yr Offeren (St Dyfrig Chapel)
11.00 am	Holy Eucharist (Lady Chapel)
6.00 pm	Evensong

Friday

9.30 am	Holy Eucharist (Lady Chapel)
5.30 pm	Evensong

Saturday

9.30 am   Choral Eucharist
6.00 pm   Evensong
Weekday Services subject to alteration,
please contact the Cathedral Office.

Bishops

982-993	Marcluith
993-1022	Bledri
1022-1059	Joseph
1059-1107	Herewald
1107-1134	Urban
vacant for 6 years	
1140-1148	Uhtred
1148-1183	Nicholas ap Gwrgant
1186-1191	William de Saltmarsh
1193-1218	Henry de Abergavenny
1219-1229	William de Goldcliff
1230-1240	Elias de Radnor
1240-1244	William de Christchurch
1245-1253	William de Burgh
1253-1256	John de la Ware
1257-1266	William de Radnor
1266-1287	William de Braose
1287-1297	Philip de Staunton or vacant
1297-1323	John de Monmouth
1323-1323	Alexander de Monmouth
1323-1347	John de Egglescliffe
1347-1361	John Paschal

1361-1382	Rodger Cradock
1383-1385	Thomas Rushook
1385-1389	William Bottlesham
1390-1393	Edmund Bromfeld
1394-1395	Robert Tideman of Winchcombe
1395-1396	Andrew Barret
1396-1398	John Burghill
1398-1407	Thomas Peverel
1408-1423	John de la Zouche
1425-1440	John Wells
1440-1458	Nicholas Ashby
1458-1476	John Hunden
1476-1478	John Smith
1478-1496	John Marshall
1496-1499	John Ingleby
1500-1516	Miles Salley
1517-1537	George de Athequa
1537-1545	Robert Holgate
1545-c.1557	Anthony Kitchin
c.1557-1560	vacant for 3 years
1560-1575	Hugh Jones
1575-1591	William Blethyn
1591-1594	Gervase Babington
1594-1601	William Morgan
1601-1618	Fraser Godwin
1618-1619	George Carleton
1619-1627	Theophilus Field
1627-1639	William Murray
1639-c.1644	Morgan Owen
1644-1660	vacant during Commonwealth
1660-1667	Hugh Lloyd

1667-1675	Francis Davies
1675-1679	William Lloyd
1679-1707	William Beaw
1707-1724	John Tyler
1724-1728	Robert Clavering
1728-1738	John Harris
1738-1740	Matthias Mawson
1740-1748	John Gilbert
1748-1754	Edward Cresset
1754-1761	Richard Newcome
1761-1769	John Ewer
1769-1769	Jonathan Shipley
1769-1782	Hon. Shute Barrington
1782-1816	Richard Watson
1816-1819	Herbert March
1819-1826	William Van Mildert
1826-1827	Charles Richard Sumner
1827-1849	Edward Copleston
1849-1882	Alfred Ollivant
1883-1905	Richard Lewis
1905-1931	Joshua Pritchard Hughes
1931-1939	Timothy Rees
1939-1957	John Morgan
1957-1971	William Glyn Hughes Simon
1971-1975	Eryl Stephen Thomas
1976-1985	John Worthington Poole Hughes
1985-1999	Roy Thomas Davies
1999-	Dr Barry Cennydd Morgan

Deans

1840-1843	John Probyn
1843-1845	William Bruce Knight
1845-1857	William Daniel Conybeare
1857-1877	Thomas Williams
1877-1879	Henry Lynch-Blosse
1879-1897	Charles John Vaughan
1897-1913	William Harrison Davey
1913-1926	Charles Edward Thomas Griffith
1926-1929	Frederick William Worsley
1929-1931	Frank Garfield Hodder Williams
1931-1948	David John Jones
1948-1954	William Glyn Hughes Simon
1954-1968	Eryl Stephen Thomas
1968-1971	Gordon Lewis Phillips
1971-1977	John Frederick Willimas
1977-1993	Alun Radcliffe Davies
1993-1999	John Rogers (Retired)
2000-2012	John Thomas Lewis

Organists

1861	John Bernard Wilkes
1866	Francis Edward Gladstone
1870	Theodore Edward Aylward
1876	Charles Lee Williams
1882	Hugh Brooksbank
1894	George Galloway Beale
1937	William Henry Gabb

1946	Albert Vernon Butcher
1949	Thomas Hallford
1950	Eric Arthur Coningsby
1955	Charles Kenneth Turner
1957	Eric Howard Fletcher
1958	Robert Henry Joyce
1974	Michael John Smith
2000	Richard Moorhouse

Sources

Llandaff Cathedral, edited by Nick Lambert, published by Seren (2010).

Around and About Llandaff Cathedral, by Dr Chrystal Davies.

Guide for Young People – All About Llandaff Cathedral, written and designed by Philip Morris (2003).

The Cathedrals, Abbeys & Priories of Wales, by Tim McCormick, pub. Logaston Press 2010.

The Organists and Organs of the Welsh Cathedrals in the 20th Century, compiled by Enid Bird, published by Enid Bird, 16 Miller Ave, Wakefield, West Yorkshire. WF2 7DJ.

The Oxford Dictionary of Saints by David Farmer, published by Oxford University Press in 1992.

Llandaff Cathedral website.

John Bethell, Llandaff Cathedral Archivist (Guided interview).

Rev. Canon Graham Holcombe (Interview)

st woolos cathedral newport

*St Woolos Cathedral in Newport finally achieved
its status as Monmouth Cathedral in 1949,
but in essence it has a history of Christian
worship going back to the early Celtic saints.*

According to legend, Gwynllyw, a 6th century
chieftain in South East Wales (Lord of Gwynllwg – a
district between the rivers Rhymney and the Usk),
founded the Church. Woolos is an English corruption of
his name. Converted to the Christian faith by St Tathan
of Caerwent, chroniclers tell how Gwynllyw was told in
a dream of how he would find a hill near a river, and
there a white ox with a black spot between its horns.
Where he found it, he was to build a church as an act of
penitence. This is thought to have been on Stow Hill in
Newport where the Cathedral Church of St Woolos now
stands, a place from which 'sea shores with plains and a
wood with lofty trees are seen extensively'.

Gwynllyw was married to Gwladys, the daughter of
the legendary Welsh king, Brychan, from whom Brecon
(Brycheiniog) gets its name. Having failed to captivate
her with his charms, he captured her through force. Her
piety and that of their son Cadoc contributed to
Gwynllyw's conversion.

His original Celtic Church of wattle and daub
construction has long ago disappeared, but the present
St Woolos on a hillock, Stow Hill, in the centre of
Newport proudly proclaims his faith. There are many

churches throughout the area founded by the family, Cadoc, Woolos' son in particular; fifteen South Wales churches are dedicated to him, including the one at Llancarfan (Nantcarfan) in the Vale of Glamorgan, a church which he founded. It is from Nantcarfan in the 11th century that Bishop Urban relocated the Canons to Llandaff to provide the Chapter for his new Cathedral there.

St Woolos's historical journey to be accepted as a fully fledged diocesan Cathedral, began following the disestablishment from the Church of England in 1920 when the Anglican Church in Wales hence-forth became known as the Church in Wales (The Church of England remained the established church in England). Two new Sees were created in 1921, that of Swansea & Brecon, and Monmouth and St Woolos at Newport was chosen for the latter as a Pro-Cathedral, a church acting as a Cathedral.

But it wasn't a walk-over. There were many other serious options including the grandiose restoration and refurbishment of Tintern Abbey, and the building of a Neo-Gothic super-structure on Newport's Ridgeway, but both of these schemes were aborted on financial grounds. Other possibilities considered were St Mary's Abergavenny, St Mary's Monmouth and St Mary's Chepstow.

The Church of St Woolos however still had over-riding considerations because, positioned prominently in Newport, Wales' third largest city (population in the 2002 census was more than 116,000), it had been dominant in the area's church life. Two of its incumbents before the creation of the Diocese of Monmouth had been Archdeacons of Llandaff. Further, the building's antiquity with its foundation going back to the earliest days of the Celtic Church bore witness to a continuity of Christian worship that few other places could match.

Once this was fully established, a decree in 1930 by the Governing Body of the Church in Wales, created a Chapter consisting of a Dean, two Archdeacons and ten Canons, with rights of presentation and patronage vested in the Bishop of Monmouth.

Thus finally, full Cathedral status was accorded in 1949.

St Woolos among the 'newer' of Wales ancient cathedrals is full of surprises. Step through the great west door, be greeted by friendly welcomers, already you're back in a 13th century Chapel. Within its primitive walls, a tomb of Sir John Morgan of Tredegar, a knight of the Holy Sepulchre (d 1491) and his wife Janet a daughter of David Matthew of Cardiff, and the tiny square windows, once mere slits and shuttered, tell us of its antiquity. CADW, Wales' guardians of our ancient heritage whilst working on a £1.5m Cathedral restoration here in 2011, have established that the roof timbers are medieval.

The following is the report which contributes greatly to our knowledge of the antiquity of St Woolos Cathedral.

Draft tree-ring dating report for Vernacular Architecture, vol. 42 (2011).

23. NEWPORT, St Wool(l)os Cathedral (ST 3090 8760)
(a) Nave roof Felling date range: 1402-32
(b) North Aisle roof Felling date·range: 1475-1505
(c) South Aisle roof Felling date range: 1487-1517
(a) Rafters (4/9) 1397(H/S), 1392(H/S), 1388(H/S), 1387(H/S). (b) Ashlars 1466(1), 1463(H/S); Rafters (0/3). (c) Arch-braces 1482, 1481(2), 1480(H/S3), 1474, 1473, 1467, 1466, 1437. Site Master (a) 1292-1397 WOOLAS1 (t = 7.7 BUTTSBNK; 7.1 WAUNMN2; 6.1 LNYWATHN); (b) 1379-1466 WOOLAS3 (t = 5.8 FORESTR1; 5.8 NHRA; 5.5 DITTON3); (c) 1318-1482 WOOLAS2 (t = 9.8 DENBY6; 9.3 WALES97; 9.2 ALWCSQ02)

St Woolos is a large multi-period urban church with a twelfth-century nave and late-fifteenth-century tower and aisles. The church was probably badly damaged during Owain Glyndŵr's revolt which laid waste the lordship of Newport in 1402/3. The nave and aisles have a complete set of late-medieval wagon roofs, but the roofs are not identical and are the result of several campaigns of renewal. The rather plain 'open' wagon roof of the nave (a) (probably boarded over the rood loft) proved to be the earliest and its date range coincides with the recovery of the town, marked by the renewal of its charter by Humphrey, Earl of Stafford, in 1427. The finer, moulded, aisle roofs (with evidence for boarding in the north aisle) belong to a late-medieval phase or phases of improvement marked by the reconstruction (widening and heightening) of the aisles and the building of the tower, the latter attributed to Jasper Tudor, lord of Newport 1485-95. The south aisle roof (c) probably belongs to the period when Edward, Duke of Buckingham, who was lord of Newport 1498-1521. His Stafford badges were formerly in the windows of this aisle. The north aisle roof (b) is probably slightly earlier. Four samples from the original chancel roof failed to date. Description in John Newman, 2000, The Buildings of Wales: Gwent/Monmouthshire, 422-28. Dating commissioned by RCAHMW with the assistance of Michael Davies, architect. NPRN 220468

Dan Miles & Richard Suggett

Canon Andrew Willie, a member of the Cathedral Chapter and Vicar of St Mark's Newport, who is the author of the cathedral's illustrated guidebook believes that the Chapel now called St Mary's, dates to around the year 1,000, and was later added to by the Normans who built the present nave. 'Subjected to raids by Nordic pirates, and marauding Saxons and even Celts, the last raid being by Earl Harold Godwinson, the last Saxon King of England, it was possibly left roofless', he says. Although roofless and maybe in ruins it seems that the Normans, probably out of respect for its holiness and antiquity, chose to preserve it.

The building was vandalised terribly by the Puritans in the 17th century. It became briefly a Presbyterian chapel: the bishops were done away with, the Medieval baptismal font was thrown out and buried. Monmouth was a strong outpost of Catholicism, and all evidence of Roman influence, by order of the Privy Council, was to be destroyed. Fortunately the old baptismal font was dug up and restored early in the 19th century, and now assumes an honourable place within the Lady Chapel. Although now mostly Victorian, its shaft and a fragment of the font basin are Norman.

In the chapel's eastern 'outer' wall there's a Norman archway which leads to the extension built later as a daughter church to Gloucester Abbey (the link with Gloucester continued until 1882). The Archway with its tapering pillars, brought here from the nearby Roman settlement at Caerleon is one of the glories of the Cathedral; Roman with Corinthian features, they speak symbolically of Noah's flood or the baptism of Jesus.

Through the arch the eye is enraptured once more by what is now the Cathedral nave and in the distance the high altar. And here a further surprise, a mural: a striking example of modern art by the artist John Piper (1903-1992), captures the eye. As is the case with many examples of contemporary art, its significance is not readily apparent. Here possibly can be discerned the Holy Spirit in tongues of fire mingled with elements of the creation and the Garden of Eden. All within a tall arch with a round stained glass window at its head. Piper employed Patrick Reyntiens to make the window: using gold and yellow colours, he interpreted it using silver stain. Appropriately, the cross is a dominant feature.

The Cathedral organ is a hybrid of earlier instruments: a combination of the old Griffin and Stroud cathedral organ, and the fine Hill organ (previously in the now demolished Newport Town Hall), which had been rebuilt by Hill, Norman and Beard in 1966. A further £200,000 makeover in 1997 by Nicholson & Company of Malvern means that the St Woolos organ has, in the words of musical director Christopher Barton, now undergone a 'completely miraculous transformation'. Sited slightly elevated behind the choir stalls with the organ pipes located opposite, it is evidently a joyous musical instrument.

The Canons' Stalls where the Cathedral Chapter (the body of clergy whose charge is to help the Dean run the Cathedral) sit, are interesting. While registering the names of the early local saints (e.g. Julius circa 304 A.D., who was martyred at Caerleon; Tewdric, king of Morganwg; Dyfrig circa 550 A.D. one of the earliest and most important of the South Wales saints (his earliest foundation was at Archenfield, Hereford; Cadoc and Gwladys, the son and wife of Gwynllyw (Woolos) respectively), the stalls are relatively recent. They were made by Robert (The Mouseman) Thompson (1876 – 1955) of Kilburn, North Yorkshire and true to form he has engraved a mouse on opposite ranks of stalls!

All that is left to remind us that there was once in the Middle Ages a Rood screen over the chancel, from which the Gospel was read, is the short stairway that leads to nowhere! That went in the 17th century purge 'on everything like that, the monuments were mutilated, the church was reduced to a traditional preaching box with high box pews'. The Puritans or their successors had them replaced with a singing gallery for a choir. St Woolos' survival given its appalling visitations, abused as a result of the Owain Glyndŵr rebellion in 1402 and later by the Cromwell insurgence, is nothing short of miraculous. Added to that, severe structural decay meant that in the 19th century the east end had to be rebuilt, and St Mary's Chapel, which had been formerly used as a charnel house, was brought back into the church.

The early 1960s once more saw reconstruction (to designs by Alban Caroe); the Victorian east end was demolished and replaced by a construction better able to accommodate the Bishop, Dean, Chapter and choir which included a number of vestries and ancillary rooms together with a processional way. Given the narrow site this was a remarkable achievement.

Discussing the influences, Canon Willie reflects on Newport and poses the question: 'Was it a Welsh city with a Welsh language in the 19th century?' 'I don't think it was', he says. 'Here we are on Stow Hill, if it was strongly Welsh it would be a "Llan". In fact, the Doomsday Book came as far as Caldicot, half way between here and Chepstow. If you went to these places forty years ago you would have found people talking with a Gloucestershire accent, that's the way it was. And then there was the arrival of steel workers from the Midlands who came to work at Llanwern!'

Steel works, coal mining, a busy port and an ancient

castle have evidently imparted their stamp. In the Cathedral there's a monument, which acknowledges the debt to one of those pioneering industrialists, Benjamin Prat, who with two other Midlands businessmen, Thomas Hill and Thomas Hawkins, was responsible for founding the Blaenavon Iron Works at the close of the 17th century. (Blaenavon Ironworks at Torfaen, a World Heritage site, is now a museum under the care of CADW). The monument may well be upside down. With the bottom turned to the top, it becomes in shape, a perfect reproduction of a lit furnace as used for smelting.

Canon Willie regards the Victorian South Porch, for much of the Cathedral's history, the main entrance, with a degree of disdain (it now functions as the cathedral shop). The original medieval porch had a room above it for a priest from Gloucester Abbey to stay. He would come to say mass, to baptise and to hear confession and stay in the room overnight.

'That has been lost because the Victorians didn't understand what it was, nor what it was for and dismissing it as a later addition, replaced it with a porch of their own', he says. 'Part of Medieval history has been lost'. The dignified south porch with the priest's room above it and the dramatically impressive tower were erected in the 15th century by Jasper Tudor, uncle of Henry VII. The bell tower houses thirteen bells, the largest peal in the whole of Wales. From the outside, the tower's elegance remains as a great welcoming colossus and up there the statue of a rather mutilated Jasper Tudor, some say as a result of gunshot from Cromwell's men, others offer the more likely explanation of weather erosion.

Music at Newport Cathedral

Donald Bates, a former Cathedral Organist at St Woolos (1964-1978), has said that no one can state for certain what music was provided for the church in earlier times and considers that on the balance of probability, in the eighteenth century the hymns were sung to violin, bass viol and flute accompaniment, or else the parish clerk would sing a line and the congregation repeat it.

In 1819 however a small organ was built and erected by Smith of Bristol, founder of Vowles & Son, and placed on a gallery known as the 'Singing Gallery'. This was at the east end of the nave over the entrance to the chancel, where there was also ample room for a large choir, the organist being a Mr Davis. In 1824 the Rev. W.W. Isaacson, an outstanding figure at St Woolos, intent on improving the standard of music produced a service book of selected psalms, hymns and anthems. It proved so popular that a second edition was produced in 1830.

In 1833, a Mr Hall of Chepstow was appointed organist, and then in 1834 T.R Price 'a much respected and efficient organist at this church' fulfilled a tenure of nineteen years. About 1840 considerable additions and improvements were made to the organ. In 1855 we learn of the church re-opening after extensive repairs and improvements – the singing gallery taken down and a new chancel erected. And at the west end of the church a special gallery to receive it. The opening service took place in 1858 with H.J. Groves now at the organ (having succeeded T.R. Price in 1853) and the 'augmented choir for that occasion sang with profound effect'.

In 1878 the organ was again moved, with additions and improvements, to the north aisle, by Mr Vowles of Bristol at a cost of approximately £500. Later a surpliced choir was introduced to lead the singing from a raised platform immediately in front of the organ. The gallery at the west end of the nave was subsequently removed and the 'Ancient and Modern' hymnal, together with 'The Cathedral Psalter' adopted.

There were further organ alterations in 1895, and in 1915 it was rebuilt by Griffen & Stroud of Bath with most of the pipes from the previous instrument incorporated into the new one. The organ was once again moved, this time to the chancel.

When the Cathedral extensions were effected in 1960 the organ was removed for two years, and a grand piano used to accompany the services.

In 1966 an organ, built by Hill, Norman and Beard which was basically a hybrid of the old Hill organ formerly in Newport Town Hall, with much of the pedal section from the Griffin & Stroud cathedral organ incorporated, was installed.

By the late 1980s the organ was in serious need of attention and an organ fund to raise the necessary £200,000 needed for a major rebuild was set up. So mission accomplished, Nicholson & Company undertook the work and 'what they achieved is incredible'. Director of Music Christopher Barton has said: 'At St Woolos we are now the proud possessors of a wonderfully versatile instrument which is truly inspirational. It will serve the cathedral, its worship and extra-liturgical musical life for generations to come. Nicholsons have achieved a completely miraculous transformation.'

Christopher Barton, Organist and Master of the Choristers since 1979, was born in London in 1956, and educated at the Royal Grammar School High Wycombe followed by Trent College, Nottingham. He then went to Worcester College, Oxford as Organ Scholar. Upon leaving Oxford he set on a teacher training course at the University of London Institute of Education, but was unable to complete the course due to his appointment to St Woolos. He studied organ with James Dalton and Richard Popplewell, and composition with Edmund Rubbra. Mr Barton's professional qualifications are M.A., F.R.C.O. (CHM), A.D.C.M., L.R.A.M. and he also holds the honorary awards and diplomas F.G.C.M., A.R.S.C.M. and A.W.A.C.M. With the Cathedral Choir he has been responsible for the music at many important provincial services, including the consecration of three bishops and the enthronement of an archbishop. When The Most Revd. Dr Rowan Williams, Archbishop of Wales, was appointed Archbishop of Canterbury, Newport Cathedral Choir was invited to sing at his enthronement in Canterbury Cathedral.

From 1985 to 1998 Christopher Barton was Music Director of the Dyfed Choir, one of the leading U.K. Mixed choirs, and he has returned several times to guest conduct them since then.

The Cathedral Choir is drawn from scholars of junior and secondary schools in and around Newport normally numbering between 16 and 20 choristers, while the gentlemen of the choir are drawn from a number of professions, teaching being particularly well represented. At any given time there are also a number of former choristers, teenage boys who now sing alto, tenor or bass. The Choirs' prime role is the maintenance of the regular sung worship at the cathedral; two services on Sundays and Choral Evensong on Wednesdays and Fridays. There is also a Training Choir for younger boys, which feeds into the main cathedral choir, and which sings services on some Mondays.

Special services are sung in Advent, at Christmas and Holy Week and at other particular times in the church calendar. In addition the choir has musical responsibility for such important occasions as Ordinations, Installations of Canons and so on. The Choir frequently performs outside its own cathedral in singing services and concerts during tours; it has sung single services or tours at most cathedrals within a radius of a hundred miles, and toured widely in the UK including five times to York Minster, Lincoln Cathedral and many others. It is a regular visitor to sing services at Westminster Abbey, and it broadcasts regularly on radio and television. Further afield, tours have been made to Ireland, Canada, Holland, Belgium and Germany (three times). The choir's repertoire is a wide one, both challenging and ambitious, ranging from plainsong to specially commissioned music from such composers as William Mathias, Herbert Sumsion, Philip Moore, Richard Shephard, Robert Ashfield, Elis Pehkonen, Adrian Williams, Simon Mold and Paul Ritchie. But it's not all work and no play, away from the choir stalls there's an active social life, with regular non-singing holidays and day trips. Christopher Barton sees these as 'very important in helping to cement the happy relationships necessary in a choir, especially one which demands so much from its choristers on a completely voluntary basis.'

The Bishop

Rt. Revd. Dominic Walker, succeeded Dr Rowan Williams as Bishop of Monmouth in 2003. Born in 1948, Bishop Dominic was educated at Plymouth College, Kings College London and Heythrop College. Following his curacy at St Faith, Southwark, he was appointed Rector of Newington St Mary, before his move to St Peter's, Brighton as Vicar and Rural Dean of Brighton. He became Bishop of Reading in 1997 up to his move to St Woolos in 2003.

The Dean

Dean Jeremy Winston was installed dean in September 2011 but was taken ill only days after his installation and was diagnosed with a brain tumour which killed him. The shock to everyone was keenly felt, especially in Abergavenny where he had been vicar for eighteen years.

His successor, now Dean of Monmouth, is **the Very Reverend Lister Tonge** who was brought up in Manchester. He studied for ordination at Kings College,

London and St Augustine's, Canterbury before serving curacies at Liverpool Parish Church and Johannesburg Cathedral. Twelve years in the Community of the Resurrection ('Mirfield Fathers') in West Yorkshire introduced him to the ministry of retreats and spiritual direction in which he spent the following thirty years.

Graduate studies in Chicago and work with ecumenical teams at home led to increasing involvement in training of others for ministry of the kind. He has worked extensively abroad, particularly with Scandinavian and Nordic Lutherans.

Employed as Chaplain to the Community of St John Baptist he was also able to be Chaplain of Ripon College Cuddesdon and, as interim, Chaplain first at New College and then at Exeter College, Oxford. He continues to be Chaplain to the CSJB Sisters in Oxford and in the United States.

Bishops

1921-28 – Charles Green, his vision of having a building of splendour built on the Ridgeway as a Cathedral for the Monmouth Diocese proved too costly.

1928-40 – Gilbert Cunningham Joyce was previously Archdeacon of Monmouth. St Woolos on Stow Hill confirmed as a Pro-Cathedral during his tenure.

1940-45 – Alfred Monahan, an Irish man became Bishop, was previously Archdeacon of Monmouth.

1945- 67 – Edwin Morris, became Archbishop of Wales in 1957-67.

1968-71 – Eryl Thomas, became Bishop of Monmouth, then in 1971 Llandaff.

1971-86 – Derrick Childs, previously Principal of Trinity College Carmarthen became Archbishop of Wales in 1983, retired in 1986 but died in the following year as the result of a car accident.

1986-91 – Clifford Wright, was previously Archdeacon of Newport.

1991-2002 – Dr Rowan Williams, previously Lady Margaret Professor of Divinity at Oxford and Canon of Christ Church. became Archbishop of Wales in 1999, then in 2002 Archbishop of Canterbury.

2003 – Dominic Walker, previously Bishop of Reading.

Deans

1929	J. R. Lloyd Jones
? -1976	Raymond Ellis Evans
1976-1990	Frank Graham Jenkins
1990-1997	Gareth Lewis
1997-2011	David Richard Fenwick
2011-2011	Jeremy Winston
2012-	Lister Tonge

Organists

1894-1934	John Augustus Gaccon
1934-1941	Cyril James Ball
1941-1963	Charles St Ervan Johns
1964-1978	Donald William Bate
1979-	Christopher Michael John Barton

St Woolos Cathedral Newport, Diocese of Monmouth

Bishop: The Right Reverend Dominic Walker.
Dean: The Very Reverend Lister Tonge.
Organist and Master of the Choristers:
Christopher Barton.
Assistant Organist: Jeremy Blasby.
The Diocesan Office, 64 Caerau Road, Newport. NP 4HJ.
Telephone: 01633 267 490 Fax: 01633 265 586
Diocesan Secretary: Ms Stella Schultz
email: stellaschultz@churchinwales.org.uk
Cathedral Website: www.churchinwales.org.uk/
monmouth/people/cathedralDeanChapter
Cathedral Choir website: www.newportcathedral-choir.org

Sunday Services

8am	Holy Eucharist
10.30 am	Sung Eucharist (Family Eucharist on the first Sunday of each month)
6.30pm	Choral Evensong (Parish Evensong normally on the second Sunday of each month)
10.00am	Sunday School in the hall except 1st Sunday, in Church

Weekday Services

Daily

8.00 am	Morning Prayer and Eucharist
10.00am	Thursday Eucharist
7.00 pm	Wednesday, Friday Choral Evensong (Wednesday boys' voices)
7.00 pm	Some Mondays Evensong (Training Choir)
5.30 pm	Other weekdays Said Evening Prayer

Sources

St Woolos Cathedral Newport – Illustrated Guide Book by Revd. Canon Andrew Willie (2nd edition Published 2002). Available from the Cathedral.

Rod Cooper, *Abbeys and Priories of Wales*, published by Christopher Davies Ltd Swansea (1993).

Enid Bird, *The Organists and Organs of the Welsh Cathedrals in the 20th Century,* published by Enid Bird, 16 Miller Ave, Wakefield, West Yorkshire. WF2 7DJ. Phone 01924 250 115.

David Hugh Farmer, *'The Oxford Dictionary of Saints,* published by Oxford University Press 1992.

St Woolos Cathedral website.

Tim McCormick, *The Cathedrals, Abbeys & Priories of Wales,* published by Logaston Press 2010.

Revd. Canon Andrew Willie, (Guided interview of Cathedral).

Christopher Barton, (article and consult).

st asaph cathedral

How Kentigern, the Scotsman, Set up a Large Monastic Order in North Wales.

Tradition has it that St Kentigern (*Cyndeyrn*), who was born and brought up in Scotland, a pupil of St Serf (Servanus) the apostle of Western Fife at Culross, became the first bishop of the locality later to be known as St Asaph. In Scotland Kentigern was known as St Mungo, a corruption of the Gaelic Munghu, Dear Pet, the name St Serf gave him. He later left his mentor and went to Glasgow where at the request of the king he was consecrated bishop in the Strathclyde area. His energetic zeal converting and reforming his people, many still pagan, however did not please the king or his successors, resulting in Kentigern having to flee to Wales.

D.R. Thomas in his 'History of the Diocese of St Asaph' says 'The first religious establishment, or monastery was founded early in the latter half of the 6th century, on the southern bank of the River Elwy by Kentigern (Cyndeyrn), the exiled bishop of the Northern Britons in Strathclyde'. His territory had extended from 'the Clyde to the Mersey and from the sea to the hills that form the watershed, and was therefore in the south practically conterminous with this diocese'.

He'd been forced by the dissensions of his countrymen to quit his Northern See in about 560 and make his way to Mynwy (Menevia), just then considered famous as the Episcopal seat of St David (Dewi Sant).

D.R. Thomas contends that 'Such a visit accords well with the oneness in race, language and creed of the Britons as far as Glasgow in the North and West Wales, and with the high reputation in which St David stood'. This is a profound statement; with our present modes of travel and communication it is no problem, but all this happened fifteen hundred years ago when conditions were very different! True the Romans had laid down an improved road system and according to D. R. Thomas, Kentigern (Cyndeyrn) would have used them. But this was ancient Britain, still primitive – probably ruled by folklore and superstition. Myth and fable prevailed, miracles 'happened'.

Having conferred with St David, Kentigern made his way northward. South-east of Carmarthen there is a church at Llangyndeyrn which is dedicated to St Kentigern. Could Kentigern have set up a monastery there before continuing his journey? This is a strong possibility because in the late nineteenth century while renovating this large ancient church, removing dilapidated pews and decayed floor-boards, an astonishing discovery was made. Beneath the nave and the aisle, an area of some 2,240 square feet, 497 skeletons of adult men were discovered. They had been tiered to a depth of five feet closely packed with their heads to the east. There were no women or children, and most surprising of all they were in perfect condition: no fractured bones or cleft skulls. Could this be the remains of a monastery founded by the Saint with skeletons of monks who had perished as the result of Yellow Fever?

And so he came to the southerly end of the Vallis

Clutina (Vale of Clwyd). A name synonymous with his native Strathclyde. The dictionary shows 'Strath' as being a Scottish noun to portray a broad valley or glen. Gaelic in origin it equates with the Irish 'srath' and Welsh 'ystrad' while the River Clwyd has a connotation with Clyde. It seems that Kentigern was fated to come here!

He found a location for his collegium on the southerly bank of the River Elwy. Here again myth and fact merge. One version of events says that Kentigern came to this region, his fame having spread to North Wales, at the invitation of Cadwallon, King of Gwynedd. Later it seems that he fell foul of King Maelgwn, Cadwallon's son, a powerful and malicious ruler of most of North Wales. Maelgwn probably saw Kentigern as some kind of threat to his sovereignty. The Christian settlement at Bangor founded by Deiniol had received his blessing but he fiercely resisted another Christian foundation at St Asaph. Legend has it that Maelgwn was struck blind and had his sight miraculously restored which resulted in his conversion. He appears to have been converted to a better mind, and to have conferred on Kentigern privileges by endowing his institution with a generous hand. Thus Maelgwn became Kentigern's ally and the See of St Asaph was affirmed.

D.R. Thomas in his treatise discusses the circumstances of how Kentigern found a suitable location for his monastery. A mistaken rendering of Welsh words seems to have led people to wrong conclusions he says, as when 'aper' (aber), the confluence of two rivers Clwyd and Elwy, where Kentigern built his institution, is treated as 'aper', a boar which led him to the spot. Similarly D.R. Thomas concludes that the reference to a 'white boar' as having acted as his guide is a misrepresentation of Berwyn (Ber Wyn), the mountain Kentigern traversed on his journey from South Wales.

We therefore conclude that a large wooden monastery was built near the River Elwy by Kentigern and his young disciple Asaph (or Asa), a local person. This must have been a huge undertaking because it accommodated 965 monks; divided into three, 300 engaged in agriculture, 300 in household duties and the remaining 365 in continuous worship 'blessing the Lord at every season'. It is difficult to comprehend the work involved: foresters and construction workers, craftsmen using wattle and daub were certainly required. Workers were needed to cultivate or hunt for food – it was all a major undertaking.

Having established a collegium, Kentigern returned to Strathclyde leaving his trusted young pupil Asaph to continue the work.

Here then began the seed of a monastery with a Bishop, at first ministering to a relatively small community. Place names within the St Asaph area show the spread of its influence: Llanasa (Asa's Church), Pant Asa(ph) (Asa's Hollow), Onnen Asa (Asa's Ash Tree) and Ffynnon Asa (Asa's Well). One of the wonders of Asaph has it that his horse left its hoof print on St Asaph High Street when it leapt there wondrously from Ffynnon Asa three miles away!

Let us now consider where the collegium on the southern bank of the River Elwy was built. Since the river flows through St Asaph from south to north before eventually joining the River Clwyd near Rhuddlan, it can't possibly have a southerly bank. But the Elwy is, a winding river which, further up country from St Asaph in the former ancient township of Wigfair it takes a gradual turn westward. Here then we have the option of a southerly bank.

Near that bend in the course of the river we find the ideal place where Kentigern may have built his monastery. It has all the requirements for a monastic life. That spot is known as Dolbelydr, now the site of a 16th century manor house restored by the Landmark Trust in 1992 from a near ruinous hulk.

Place names, geographical features, and folklore are all factors to take into account in our search for the lost monastery. Dolbelydr sometimes called Ffynnonfer is on the south bank of the River Elwy as it gradually veers westward . In a field on the opposite side of the river, some three hundred yards distance, there's a well – Ffynnon Fair (Ffynnonfer is also the way the old folk talked of the old Tudor house, reflecting an association with the well). Ffynnon Fair is Welsh for Mary's Well. Lady Margaret Beaufort, the mother of King Henry VII, is believed to have been responsible for erecting the church there, now a ruin, and a baptismal bath. Miracle cures for blindness and infertility were considered features of the water which still gushes forth at 4000 gallons an hour, its temperature constant. It's been for long a shrine of pilgrimage, poets such as Gerard Manley Hopkins, Felicia Hemans and Sion Tudur have been enraptured. This is an evidently sacred and beautiful place. Although the church may date to the 14th century, the well pre-dating it, could easily have been a feature of Celtic/British worship in the 5th/6th century.

In making a case for the location of Kentigern's monastery as being where Dolbelydr/Ffynnonfer now stands, it is necessary to probe further. Dolbelydr as a place name is open to various meanings and is clearly a combination of two words: dôl is the Welsh word for meadow; pelydr is ray, as in for example, a sun's rays – a sun beam. We then have the vision of the morning sun's rays shimmering on a beautiful riverside meadow. Another definition offered is that pelydr could translate as pellitory, a plant that might easily have been cultured by the monks for culinary or medicinal purposes.

A short distance from here, near Glan Llyn Farm, there is a bend in the river, where by nature or design, a pool has been created. Professor Hywel Wyn Owen the leading UK authority on place names reasons that 'Wigfair' (up to late 19th century a township) where the well, Dolbelydr and this part of the river is located, could be defined as 'fish farm'. This locality was once referred to by the native inhabitants as Wickwer: as a generality 'wick' or 'wich' in a place name indicates a farm, while 'were' as in this instance refers to 'weir', a trap in the river to catch fish. We can then deduce that the pool at Glanllyn may have been once used as a fish reservoir stocked and replenished by the weirs on the river. All this would add up to a good source of food supply for the monks in the nearby monastery, while the well later dedicated to Mary (the Virgin) could be their place of meditation and spiritual renewal.

Does this proposition stand up? Circumstantially, yes it does. There are place names in the vicinity containing the name Asaph indicating that he was working his mission in this area. And although this is possibly three miles from the centre of St Asaph, we can safely assume that Wigfair/Wicwer was well within its perimeter. For instance the 17th century Welsh bard Sion Tudur in his old age claimed:

'Tario yng nghornel Llanelwy
Heb allu mynd i bell mwy'

(I tarry in the corner of Llanelwy (St Asaph),
unable to go far anymore).

And further according to 'Y Cwtta Cyfarwydd', Peter Roberts's minute book of the period it is noted that:

'upon Easter Eve, being the iiith day of Aprill anno D'ni 1602 John Tuder of Wickwer died and was buried in the parish Church of St Asaph ...'

Not only did John Tuder (Sion Tudur) of Wickwer consider that he lived in a corner of St Asaph but he died there too!

Furthermore Peter Roberts records that clandestine marriages were solemnized in the church at St Mary's Well by clergymen from St Asaph. In short we can conclude that this area due south of St Asaph has always been closely linked with St Asaph – stones for building the cathedral were quarried there at Cefn Meiriadog, the bishops relaxed in the woods hunting the squirrel at 'Coed yr Esgob' (Bishop's Wood). Indeed a 1607 memo regards residents of the present parishes of Cefn Meiriadog and St George as being parishioners of St Asaph. Interestingly Tristan Grey Hulse has identified 'Meiriadog' as being a monk/missionary from the collegium. And moreover the discoveries of human remains in the Bontnewydd Cave by Dr Stehen Green in 1978, which date back 225,000 years, are regarded as those of St Asaph's earliest inhabitants!

Coming back now to Asaph, John Fisher and Baring Gould tell us that according to Jocelin "Asaph, probably a native of Tegeingl in northern Flintshire, was 'distinguished by birth', and it may be observed that he was a nephew of Saint Dunawd, founder of the monastery at Bangor on Dee, and a cousin of Saint Deiniol, founder and first bishop of Bangor". According to Fisher and Baring Gould in 'Lives of British Saints' both St Deiniol and St Asaph were direct descendants of St Pabo king/chieftain of northern Britain, while Saint Dunawd was one of Pabo's sons.

When quite a boy he (Asaph) was placed as a disciple under Saint Kentigern, the exiled bishop of the Britons of Strathclyde, at his college on the Elwy, founded in 560. It became so famous 'that the number of those who enlisted in the army of God amounted to 965, who professed in act and manner the monastic rule according to the institution of the holy man'.

137

'Nobles and men of the middle class brought their children to the Saint to be brought up in the nurture of the Lord'. Even so John Fisher and Baring Gould have to admit that 'most of what is known about St Asaph is gleaned from the Lives of St Kentigern, especially that by Jocelin, a monk in Furness writing around 1180'. Referring to his election and consecration, it speaks of 'the sweetness of his conversation, the symmetry, vigour, and elegance of his body, the virtues and sanctity of his heart, and the manifestation of his miracles'. One such miracle shows Asaph's total trust in his mentor when Kentigern, following his customary daily reading of the Psalter in ice cold water, feeling intensely cold, ordered the youngster to bring him burning coals in order to get warm. This the lad did with no thought for himself, and not having a suitable container, begged the servant to place the burning coals in the garment he was wearing. This was done, thinking it would teach him a lesson, but Asaph successfully took the burning coals to Kentigern without injury to himself or damage to his clothing. This old Celtic legend is recorded in the Kentigern/Asaph window on the north side of the Cathedral.

The story of developments at St Asaph are unclear, but it appears that the Cathedral became bleak and impoverished. Subjected to constant raids by Picts and Norsemen, the Canons lived in fear of living in the area. St Asaph was on the direct route-path of the marauders. For some 500 years after the death of Asaph, the clergy elected their own bishops but no records remain to illuminate the period. It was the Norman Conquest of

1066 which was eventually to relieve the gloom and desolation.

Briefly

A.D.

560 Foundation of See by Kentigern (Cyndeyrn) from Strathclyde and building Monastery/Cathedral on south bank of River Elwy.

Locating the Lost Monastery.

570 Asaph, Kentigern's favourite disciple appointed Bishop.

600-1100 St Asaph – The Forgotten Years.

Notable events in the history of St Asaph Cathedral. After 1066!

This was when Welsh Sees came within the rule of Canterbury and a system of dioceses and parishes introduced. We see Archbishop Baldwin of Canterbury in the company of Giraldus Cambrensis/Gerald the Welshman touring Wales ostensibly to promote this (as well as recruiting for the Crusades) in 1188. They visited St Asaph Cathedral and celebrated mass there, noting 'the poor little church of the See of Llanelwy'.

The question now arises as to where the Cathedral was located at this time; was it on the present site? Perhaps this we shall never know for certain. If it had come up from its riverside location, the next question is, when, why and under what circumstances? The general opinion is that the cathedral was possibly positioned on its present site, believed to be the former old Roman fort of Vare, sometime after the Roman withdrawal. The when and how of its transition from a roughly hewn wooden Celtic monastery/settlement on to a prime elevated site must be left to the imagination because no records now remain to enlighten us.

The first fully substantiated Bishop of St Asaph in this 'new period' was Gilbert (consecrated in the chapel at Lambeth by Theobold, Archbishop of Canterbury) followed by Geoffrey of Monmouth in 1152 who was non-resident. He is best known for promoting the Arthurian legend. Next came Reyner who was consecrated by Archbishop Baldwin.

Bishop Hugh 1235-40 began to rebuild the Cathedral in stone (some of his efforts have survived in the gables and buttresses at the west front). In 1247 'King Henry 3rd, having conquered all Wales and brought the Welsh under the laws of England, the Welsh bishops siding with their countrymen against the king, had their Bishoprics and Churches so spoiled and destroyed that they were forced to beg for their bread and live upon the alms of others'. Henry III thus exercised the Royal Prerogative in the election of Bishops and Anian (Einion) became Bishop of St Asaph in 1249. Anian was succeeded briefly by John who was followed by Anian II in 1268. This effectively is where the history of the present Cathedral begins.

Anian II 1268-93, his effigy and tomb is in the south aisle, was a politically active bishop who , walking a tight rope, received certain privileges from Llewelyn Prince of Wales and further ones from Edward I confirming the rights of the church, and from the Earl of Arundel a hundred acres to the See conditional on the Bishop (and his successors' support). Anian also disputed and won from Vale Crucis Abbey, patronage of several parish churches including Llangollen, Wrexham, Rhuabon and Chirk.

In 1282 the Cathedral and Canons' houses were burnt to the ground by the English in their wars with the Welsh.

This resulted briefly in Anian being deprived of his bishopric which was handed over to the Bishop of Bath and Wells. In 1284 as a result of Archbishop Peckham's visit to St Asaph, consultation with Anian II and representation to the King stating that Anian had not been undutiful to the King and that the Diocese St Asaph needed a resident Bishop, Anian was reinstated.

These were turbulent times, King Edward I and the Bishop wanted the Cathedral rebuilt at Rhuddlan where its treasures could be safely guarded by the military at the Castle – the king was prepared to contribute 1000 marks towards the cost. Letters were sent to Pope Martin seeking permission to do so, but his death before a decision was taken meant that the move was not approved. This was the 'official' stance but it can be equally argued that it was by the Archbishop of Canterbury's intervention that the re-building commenced on the original site.

Let us now consider further certain historical events. In 1284, Bishop Anian now returned from exile, sets about rebuilding the Cathedral, and the 'Euaggulthen' – the 'Book of Gospels' is carried about through certain Dioceses by sanction of Archbishop Peckham to raise subscriptions for the restoration. A hundred years later we find work still in progress, but the Cathedral remains in poor order.

In 1402 the Cathedral is again burnt down and utterly destroyed by the Welsh patriot Owain Glyndŵr, and remains in ruins for nearly 80 years.

Bishop of St Asaph John Trevor, a man of great scholarship, piety and immense political ambition had supported Henry Bolingbroke, the usurper, in his deposition of Richard 2nd in 1399. This had displeased Owain Glyndŵr, who after punishing his English enemies decided to punish the Welsh who had supported Bolingbroke who was by then King Henry IV. This was the reason why Glyndŵr attacked St Asaph, set fire to the Cathedral and ravaged the Bishop's Palace and houses of the Canons. This led to Bishop Trevor changing his allegiance and by 1404 he was reconciled with Glyndŵr – but unfortunately by then the Cathedral lay in ruins.

In 1482 Bishop Redman began re-roofing the Cathedral and refitting the interior.

1534 the Dean and Chapter renounce Papal Supremacy.

1556 Bishop Thomas Gladwell, makes arrangements for improvements of the choral services.

1588 is a date forever seared in Welsh memory, when Bishop William Morgan, then Vicar of Llanrhaeadr ym Mochnant, published his translation of the Bible into Welsh (a first edition of which can be viewed at the Cathedral). He was Bishop of St Asaph from 1601 until his death in 1604. Tradition has it that he was buried inside the Cathedral near the bishop's throne and sanctuary. Further improvements of the interior together with repairs to the tower and belfry were undertaken during Bishop John Owen's tenure from 1631, but in 1646 we see further desecration by Oliver Cromwell's parliamentarians. On the appointment in 1660 of Bishop George Griffith, we see partial repairs, continued by Bishop Isaac Barrow (1669). In 1714, a violent storm blows down the upper section of the tower, causing great damage to the interior, which incurs a cost of £600 on necessary repairs. The reparation work on the tower is distinctly visible to this day.

31st of July 1774 sees Dr Samuel Johnson and Mrs Hester Thrale attending service at the Cathedral. 'The Cathedral though not large has something of dignity and Grandeur', Johnson was later to recall. 'And the Quire has, I think thirty two stalls, of antique workmanship. The constitution I do not know but it has all the usual titles and dignities. The service was sung only in the Psalms and hymns. The Bishop was very civil. We went

to his palace, which is but mean. They have a library ...'
The Mediaeval 'stalls of antique workmanship' seen by
Dr Johnson are still there, unique survivors of many
troubled times at the Cathedral.

In 1780 the Cathedral undergoes many alterations,
and the ruined Chapter House is pulled down. 1822
Lewis Wyatt consulted, who covers the whole building
with stucco.

1830 Additions made to the Bishop's Palace by Bishop
Carey , and Deanery rebuilt by Dean Luxmore.

1868 Thorough restoration of the whole Cathedral
decided upon and work begun by the architect Gilbert
Scott, later Sir George Gilbert Scott. Completed in 1875.

*George Gilbert Scott (1811-1878) was 'the
most celebrated architect in the land' when
he began work at St Asaph Cathedral in
1863. At the same time he was responsible
for the Albert Memorial (1862-63). and later
St Pancras Station and Hotel in London
(1865). He travelled all over Britain, at first
designing workhouses, then building and
restoring churches. Almost 500 during his
career as well as 39 minsters and
cathedrals. His passion was for the Gothic.
Scott never turned down a job: as an
obituarist was to say, 'He was indefatigable
in business and a fervent worker. No chance
was ever missed, no opportunity neglected'.*

April 25, 1889 Dr A. G. Edwards enthroned as Bishop –
later to be first Archbishop of Wales in 1920 when the
Church became 'disestablished'. April 22, 1892 sees the
erection of a memorial in the Cathedral forecourt to
William Morgan and his team of translators, taking the
form of a lantern.

*The Bishop Morgan Memorial, now better
known as the Translators Memorial, is an
octagonal monument standing 30 feet high
between the Cathedral and the High Street,
sited where the old Cathedral Cross once
stood. In the form of a lantern with a cross
at its apex, it follows the general design of
the late 13th century Eleanor Crosses. The
divines associated with William Morgan
are all remembered on the column : he is
featured facing the street, while from left to
right we have Richard Davies, translator of
a portion of the New Testament 1567, Bishop
of St Asaph (1560-1561), then of St David
(1561-1581); William Salesbury,who in 1551
published a Welsh translation of the
liturgical Epistles and Gospels, and was
also author of a Latinized Welsh version of
the New Testament 1567; Thomas Huet,
Presentor of St David, translated
Revelation; Richard Parry (d 1623),
succeeded Bishop Morgan to the See of St
Asaph. He revised the earlier translations*

and brought out the standard Welsh version in 1620; John Davies (d 1644), Rector of Mallwyd in Merioneth, assisted Bishop Parry; Edmund Prys, Archdeacon of Merioneth, translated the Psalms into Welsh verse; Gabriel Goodman, Dean of Westminster was a native of Ruthin in the Vale of Clwyd, a supporter of Bishop Morgan and a generous benefactor of his home town.

It is of interest to note that in the latter part of the 20th century, the north transept was refurbished to become the Translators' Chapel where a copy of the William Morgan Bible may be seen and where the weekly Welsh Eucharist services are held.

When the New Welsh Bible, Y Beibl Cymraeg Newydd, was published in 1988, commemorating the 400th Aniversary of Morgan's Bible, John Charles, Bishop of St Asaph from 1971-82 contributed to it by translating part of the Book of Esther and Paul's First Epistle to the Corinthians.

In 1915 and again in 1923 there was further concern about the structure of the Cathedral and although minor work to secure the tower was undertaken in 1915 this was found to be insufficient. Cracks appeared in the south transept and glass began to fall out of the windows. Dean J. C. Du Buisson immediately contacted

C. M. Oldrid Scott (grandson of Sir George who had fifty years earlier carried out major restoration work). His report was not good news for Du Buisson and his team: £14,000 was required to save the tower and Cathedral, a tremendous sum in a time of national economic crisis. However by 1933 the money had been found and the work completed; in a celebration on May 1st and 2nd of that year Archbishop Alfred Edwards was able to thank the Cathedral team for a magnificent achievement, the work had cost £13,954 and had been fully subscribed.

Making Music at the Cathedral

The earliest mention of an organ in St Asaph Cathedral is of an instrument replaced in 1512 and there's further reference to an organ here around 1534 when £40 was donated under the will of Bishop Henry Standish. Both Robert Dallam and Bernard Smith (Formerly Schmidt who came from Halle and built organs for Westminster Abbey and St Paul's Cathedral) worked on the instrument throughout the seventeenth century, with a new organ being constructed by Abraham Jordan in 1741. This does not preclude the possibility of an even earlier one, because organs in cathedrals since the eleventh century have been instanced in other places.

In 1834 a new instrument by William Hill was installed, consisting of two manuals, possibly with pedal pipes. In 1846 a Choir department and Pedals were added, and in 1847 new keyboards were acquired for the

Great and Swell. The organ was sited on a stone screen under the western tower arch.

In 1859 the organ was further enlarged with the addition of a short compass Swell. The Pedal compass was also increased and several mechanical alterations made. 1867 saw the removal of the stone screen and the instrument was sited on a platform in the North transept. In 1897 the organ was rebuilt and enlarged by William Hill and Son. Pneumatic action , a Solo manual and various other ranks were added.

Thirty years later the Cathedral organist Dr Harold Carpenter Lumb Stocks (1884-1956) donated an Acoustic Bass 32' stop for inclusion in the Pedal department and an electric blower was added (the work undertaken by Hill, Norman and Beard).

In 1932 the Cathedral tower was deemed unsafe so the organ was dismantled and stored while the building was made structurally sound. When the instrument was re-installed it remained totally unaltered but was given a revised eight foot case front. Hill, Norman and Beard oversaw the 1966 rebuild. Many of the original Hill stops remained, however there were several new additions. Various ranks were re-voiced whilst some pipework was discarded. The instrument was given an electric action and was reduced to three manuals with 48 speaking stops. The console was re-positioned opposite the organ case on the south side of the tower.

A £250,000 rebuild was undertaken by Wood of Huddersfield in 1998 with as much as possible of the original Hill instruments restored, providing a versatile specification to perform works from as many different styles and periods as possible. A new oak case, designed by David Graebe was constructed, the console re-instated in the organ gallery and a fourth manual incorporated into the scheme.

The present Musical Director Alan MacGuiness came to St Asaph Cathedral as an Assistant Organist in 1998 and resolved to enlarge the choir to include a girls section in addition to the boys (and men) that already existed. Five years later Alan MacGuiness was appointed Director of Music, a full time member of Cathedral staff.

He was born in 1975 and began studying the organ at the age of fourteen whilst a pupil at Liverpool's Blue Coat School. He continued his studies at The Royal Northern College of Music Manchester, where he was a prize-winner, graduating in 1997 with B.Mus (Hons). During this time his tutor was Margaret Phillips, and he also performed in many master-classes given by artists such as Dame Gillian Weir, David Sanger and David Briggs.

In September 1997 he became an Organ Scholar at Liverpool's Metropolitan Cathedral where he was influenced by Mervyn Cousins (now with Llangollen International Eisteddfod).

His first duties at St Asaph included accompanying the Cathedral Choir on the recently restored four manual Hill organ and assisting with training the choristers. Recalling first impressions he says, 'The moment I came here I felt I really wanted to play that organ'. He was impressed by the warm tone and the new oak case by David Graebe, 'the best case designer in the UK, which is why the sound is so beautiful'.

He is in demand as a recitalist, having performed at Liverpool's Anglican Cathedral, the city's St George's Hall and Blackburn Cathedral.

In August 1999 he completed a successful recital tour of New York City and New England, where the venues included the Jesuit church of St Ignatious Loyala, St Agnes Cathedral and St Patrick's Cathedral.

In January 2004 at the age of 28, he was appointed Organiser and Master of the Choristers, overseeing the musical life of the Cathedral at St Asaph. He has directed the Cathedral Choirs in both live and recorded broadcasts for national radio and television, including the BBC's Songs of Praise.

Children from 17 schools along the coast (from Colwyn Bay to Holywell and St Asaph to Chester) plus lay clerks form the Cathedral's singing contingent. The rehearsals take place in the freshly adapted offices, once used as the Diocesan headquarters. The move there came when new purpose built offices to conduct Cathedral business were constructed within the cathedral precinct. It's an arrangement that's working out surprisingly well. The main rehearsal room adequately accommodates a grand piano and all that MacGuiness needs to instruct the children. Pictures adorn the room, carefully selected to inspire the songsters: former musical directors like the long serving Drs Stocks and Middleton as well as the renowned Welsh composer William Mathias. An adjoining room is for robing, while further along there's an office which also doubles for auditions. Here also, along a side wall, there are neat shelves of 150 boxes of catalogued musical compositions.

Here too MacGuiness can give one-to-one tuition.

When choir vacancies occur the schools are informed so that children of a musical disposition can come forward for audition: boys from about seven years of age, while girls are considered from eleven. What Alan MacGuiness is looking for are children with potential: a voice and a musical ear is essential. He will strike a note on the piano and see if the child can match it. The other main requirements are that they are good readers (some of the hymns and psalms have unusual words they may not have heard before), and he's also looking for energy and commitment. Previous experience is not a condition, 'because they will get all the training here'. They will learn to read music, some may go on to play a musical instrument , enthused by what they get here. 'A lot of the choristers play the piano, violin and oboe – we've got a harpist. They can get the music bug. If they play a musical instrument, it helps with their notation. Its a whole musical education. The demand for the choir is quite high, because they don't get that musical education in schools any more', he says.

Boys coming in at seven or eight years old, after a probationary period, will normally stay until their voices change. Girls start at about eleven years old and stay until they go away to college.

The teaching sessions are after their school hours; the boys come in on Mondays and Tuesdays from 4.30 to 6 and then sing evensong until 6.45 in the Cathedral. The girls attend on Wednesdays and Fridays and follow an identical curriculum. The lay clerks, traditionally men, join in rehearsals on Mondays and Fridays. 'Normally

40 minutes before the service we rehearse in the Cathedral, to get the balance right'. This is in addition to concerts, broadcasts, weddings or funerals in which they may be asked to take part.

The Assistant Organist, a part-time role since September 2004, is John Hosking. Born in 1976, he studied the organ with Peter Jolley and David Briggs and at the age of 18 was awarded the Organ Scholarship at the Royal Parish Church of St Martin-in-the-Fields in London. Meanwhile winning the Robert Shaw Exhibition from the Royal College of Organists to study with Martin Baker.

A student at the Royal College of Music from 1995-1999, in 1996 he was appointed Organ Scholar of Westminster Abbey during which time he accompanied the Abbey Choir on State occasions.

Before his St Asaph appointment John Hosking worked at Lincoln and Truro Cathedrals and Brandean School in Exeter. A popular recitalist, he has performed in Songs of Praise and Morning Worship for the BBC.

In a discussion about the important part music plays in the life of the Cathedral mention must be made of its being the home of the 'North Wales Music Festival' held annually at the end of September since its foundation in 1972. Inspired during the tenure of Dean Raymond Renowden and the charismatic Dr William Mathias, it continues to draw world class musicians who exploit to the full its magnificent acoustics. This has led to the Cathedral becoming the ideal venue for classical concerts,and a particular favourite with male voice choirs, leading soloists and instrumentalists.

The Cathedral:
Its Part in 'Schooling and Educating'

D. R. Thomas in his 'History of the Diocese of St Asaph' refers to charities for 'schooling and educating poor children and clothing poor people of this parish' in 1729. The chief donor was a Mrs Elizabeth Williams who had left in trust to the vicars several lands and tenements in St Asaph and Tremeirchion known as Waen Farm for this purpose. A further endowment which included a sum of almost £500 left by Bishop Barrow in 1680 together with other donations made up a substantial amount in total.

The Almshouses which were founded by Bishop Barrow in 1680 received a bequest of £140 from Bishop Tanner in 1745 and were rebuilt by Bishop Bagot in 1795. These housed eight widows appointed by the Bishop, the Dean and the families of Cefn (Plas yn Cefn) and Llannerch Hall.

The Cathedral interest in the Grammar School has always been an intimate one claims D. R. Thomas; Bishop Barrow bequeathed £200 towards it in 1680 and intended, had he lived, to have built a School-house. The Grammar School was at first probably held in some part of the Cathedral, but in 1638 'a Schoolhouse roome or loft was made and finished in the lower ende of the p'ishe churche, by Edward ap Ie'un, Dafydd and others' (Peter Roberts in Y Cwtta Cyfarwydd). At a later date it was held in the Chapter House and later still in the Cathedral Close 'until the present School room was built in 1780'. About 1818 it was merged in a National School and shortly afterwards its status as a Grammar School changed to 'a rather good Commercial School, in which twenty-four boys from the parish are educated free, in consideration of the £35 per ann. added by the Vicars to the special endowments'. Writing in the mid-1870's D. R. Thomas described the school as 'consisting of one large room and a class-room; but there is no accommodation for Master or for boarders. The appointment of the Master lies with the Vicars, an office presently held by W. Easterby, Esq., LL.D. London'. At this time a 'Commission of Enquiry into the Endowed Schools of North Wales' was in session considering a proposal to convert it into a Latin or secondary school. Also under local consideration was the parochial charities, looking to increase the endowment and revive its role as a Grammar School. It is of interest to observe that the school in question is now a private house known as Bryn Afon located near the end of Mill Street. The school moved to the Upper Denbigh Road site across the road from the Cathedral in August1881. In 1889, under the terms of the Intermediate Education Act for Wales, the diocesan board was replaced by 15 elected governors and the school was one of 17 endowed grammar schools adopted as county schools. Thus Bishop Isaac Barrow's vision came to its ultimate fruition. The school's progress has been well told by Michael Hoy in his book 'Isaac Barrow: His Life and Legacy' and how finally in 1969 it housed the first Welsh Language Comprehensive School (Ysgol Glan Clwyd) in Wales with over a thousand pupils. Its association with the Cathedral continues to be a close one with a Harvest Thanksgiving and Christmas Carol

Service being a regular feature of school life.

D. R. Thomas also records 'that a handsome new National School, with its rooms for Boys and Girls, Class-room and Master's House, was erected, in 1863, at a cost of about £1,800, on a site near the Cathedral , in lieu of the previous schools which had been built in 1831; and which the boy's school has been converted to cottages, and the Girls' school is now known as the Infants School'. This school known as the VP Infants School continued to function there until the mid-1950s (sited on what is now the Cathedral Car Park) when it moved across the road to join the Junior School. The 'Junior School' later moved to a newly built one called Ysgol Esgob Morgan which is down Heol Esgob off the 'Roe', while the infants school stayed near the Cathedral.

A significant development at St Asaph at the close of the 19th century was building the Dean's Library, paid for by the then Dean Herbert Watkin Williams (Dean 1892-1899 and later Bishop of Bangor 1899-1925). His dream was 'that it should please God, to give increase to the functions of the Cathedral, a college of some sort where candidates, Deacons or Priests might study or a school of music established'.

According to his biographer, Dean Raymond Renowden,'the building was used for some time for conferences, for ordination of candidates and for choir instruction' but hardly in the long term fulfilling Dean Williams's great vision. It was left to a later dean, Raymond Renowden (1971-92), to restore its potential as a useful public facility, well used by the Cathedral and the city in general.

The Dean of St Asaph

In 2011, Dean The Very Revd Christopher Potter having served as Dean of St Asaph and Team Rector of the Rectorial Benefice of St Asaph since 2001, relinquished his role and was appointed Archdeacon of St Asaph in succession to The Venerable Bernard Thomas who was retiring. Formerly a craftsman woodworker Dean Potter, a graduate of Leeds University, lived and worked in the Diocese of St Asaph, before training for ordination within the Diocese. Following his ordination in St Asaph Cathedral in 1993, he served as Curate of Flint (1993-96), and Vicar of Llanfair Dyffryn Clwyd, Derwen and Efenechtyd from 1996 to 2001.

The Rev. Nigel Williams was installed as Dean of St Asaph Cathedral on 17th September 2011. The new Dean, a fluent Welsh speaker, was born in St Asaph and brought up in Llansannan, before training for the priesthood at St Michael's College Llandaff and the University of Wales, Cardiff.

Ordained in St Asaph Cathedral in the mid 1990s Nigel Williams served in the parishes of Denbigh & Nantglyn, Llanrwst and Llanddoged before taking up his ministry at Colwyn Bay, where between 2004 and 2009, he served as Area Dean of Rhos.

The Bishop of St Asaph

Bishop Gregory Cameron was enthroned as the 76th Bishop of St Asaph on Saturday 25 April 2009.

The Rt Revd Dr Gregory Cameron was born in South East Wales, grew up in the village of Llangybi near Usk in Monmouthshire, and educated at Croesyceiliog Comprehensive. As a teenager he discovered his faith and started attending the local Anglican Church (St Cybi). He received a vocation for the ordained ministry while reading Law at Oxford University and upon being accepted an ordinand of the Church in Wales, began a degree in Theology in Cambridge, where he was taught early church history by the young Rowan Williams. Following studies at St Michael's College, Llandaff, Gregory Cameron was ordained in the Diocese of Monmouth, serving in the Parish of St Paul, Newport, and then in the Rectorial Benefice of Llanmartin. Subsequently, he undertook ministry as a school chaplain (Wycliffe College, Stonehouse) and as director of an educational charity (The Bloxham Project). In 2000, Rowan Williams, by then Archbishop of Wales, appointed Gregory as his Chaplain.

In 2003, he was appointed Director of Ecumenical Affairs at the Anglican Communion Office in London, becoming, a year later, Deputy Secretary General. In this role, he has been involved in the ecumenical relations of the Anglican Communion at a global level, and responsible for staffing the Lambeth Commission, which produced the Windsor Report. He was granted an honorary Doctorate of Divinity by the Episcopal Divinity School, Massachusetts, in 2007, in recognition of his contribution to reconciliation in the Anglican Communion. He has lectured in Old Testament at St Michael's College, Llandaff, and is currently an Honorary Research Fellow in Canon Law at the Centre for Law and Religion in Cardiff University.

Married to Clare, who is a teacher of music and a composer, they have three sons. Gregory Cameron enjoys reading, drawing and calligraphy and is a keen Egyptologist. He is a Welsh learner, attending the local Welsh language class, and an Eisteddfod enthusiast: but six years of living in England have blunted his conversational skills! In all his ministry, he has sought to communicate the Gospel of Jesus Christ in fresh and exciting ways, and believes that the Christian faith offers hope as well as a profound challenge to the world.

St Asaph Cathedral

Bishop of St Asaph: The Rt Revd Gregory Cameron.
Dean of St Asaph: The Very Revd Nigel Williams.
Director of Music: Mr Alan McGuinness.
Cathedral Office: High St , St Asaph. LL17 0RD
Tel. 01745 582 245
e-mail: pamelathompson@churchinwales.org.uk
Website: www.churchinwales.org.uk/asaph/cathedral

Times of Services

Sundays:

8.00am	Holy Eucharist
11.00am	Choral Eucharist
3.30pm	Evening Prayer (1st, 3rd and 5th Sundays) or Choral Evensong (2nd and 4th Sundays)

The Cathedral closes at 4.00pm on Sundays.

Daily – except Sunday:

9.00am	Morning Prayer
6.00pm	Evening Prayer (Choral Evensong on Fridays in term-time)

Monday:

9.30am	Holy Eucharist
6.00pm	Choral Evensong* (*during term-time)

Wednesday:

10.30am	Holy Eucharist

Friday:

9.30am	Cymun Bendigaid

St Asaph Cathedral Organists

1620	John Day
1630	Abednigo D. Perkins
1631	John Wilson

1669	Thomas Ottey
1680	William Key
1686	Thomas Hughes
1694	Alexander Gerard
1738	John Gerard
1782	John Jones
1785	Edward Bailey
1791	Charles Spence
1794	Henry Hayden
1834	Robert Augustus Atkins
1889	Llewelyn Lloyd
1897	Hugh Percy Alien
1898	Archibald Wayet Wilson
1901	Cyril Bradley Rootham
1902	William Edward Belcher
1917	Harold Carpenter Lumb Stocks
1956	Robert Duke Dickinson
1962	James Roland Middleton
1970	Graham John Elliot
1981	John Theodore Belcher
1985	Hugh Davies
1998	Graham Eccles
2004	Alan McGuinness

Bishops of St Asaph

560	St Kentigern (Cyndeyrn)
573	St Asaph
c600	Tysilio
c800	Renchidus

c928	Cebur
c1070	Melanus
1143	Gilbert
1152	Geoffrey of Monmouth
1154	Richard
1160	Geoffrey
1175	Adam
1183	John
1186	Reiner
1225	Abraham
1235	Hugh
1240	Hywel ab Ednyfed Fychan
1247-49	vacant
1249	Anian 1 or Einion ap Meredydd
1267	John 2
1268	Anian 2 or Einion ab Ynyr
1293	Llewelyn ab Ynyr (de Bromfield)
1315	Dafydd ap Bleddyn
1346	John Trevor (Trevaur)
1357	Llywelyn ap Madog
1376	William Spridlington
1382	Laurence Child
1390	Alexander Bache
1395	John Trevor (Trevour)
1411	Robert Lancaster
1433	John Lowe
1444	Reginald Peacock
1451	Thomas Bird (alias) Knight
1471	Richard Redman
1496	Michael Deacon
1500	Dafydd ab Ieuan ab Iorwerth

1504	Dafydd ab Owen
1513	Edmund Birkhead
1518	Henry Standish
1536	Robert Wharton or Parfew
1555	Thomas Goldwell
1560	Richard Davies
1561	Thomas Davies
1573	William Hughes
1601	William Morgan
	(Translated the Bible into Welsh
1604	Richard Parry
1624	John Hanmer
1629	John Owen
1651-60	vacant
1660	George Griffith
1667	Henry Glemham
1670	Isaac Barrow
1680	William Lloyd
1692	Edward Jones
1703	George Hooper
1704	William Beveridge
1708	William Fleetwood
1715	John Wynne
1727	Francis Hare
1732	Thomas Tanner
1736	Isaac Madox
1744	Samuel Lisle
1748	Robert Hay Drummond
1761	Richard Newcome
1769	Jonathan Shipley
1789	Samuel Halifax

1790	Lewis Bagot
1802	Samuel Horsley
1806	William Cleaver
1815	John Luxmoore
1830	William Carey
1846	Thomas Vowler Short
1870	Joshua Hughes
1889	Alfred George Edwards
	(First Archbishop of Wales 1920-34)
1934	William Thomas Havard
1950	David Daniel Bartlett
1971	Harold John Charles
1982	Alwyn Rice Jones
	(Archbishop of Wales 1991-99)
1999	John Stewart Davies
2009	Gregory Cameron

Deans of St Asaph

1210	Ithel
1223	David de Witinton
1239	Robert
1244	David
1279	Anian
1305	Llewelyn
1307	Anian
1339	Llewelyn ap Madoc*
1357	Robert de Walsham
1357	William de Spridlington*
1376	Alan de Stokes

1381	Howel ap Madoc Kyffin
1397	Hugh Collingham
1402	Richard Courteney*
1404	Hugh Holbecke
1418	John Blodwel
1441	David Blodwel
1462	John Tapton Shadrach Price
1511	Fulke Salisbury
1543	Richard Puskin
1556	John Griffith
1558	Maurice Blayne
1559	John Lloyd
1560	Hugh Evans
1587	Thomas Banks
1634	Andrew Morris
1653-1660	vacant
1660	David Lloyd
1663	Humphrey Lloyd *
1673	Nicholas Stratford*
1689	George Bright
1696	Daniel Price
1706	William Stanley
1731	William Powell
1751	William Herring
1774	William Davies Shipley
1826	Charles Scott Luxmore
1854	Charles Butler Clough
1859	Richard B Maurice Bonner
1886	Herbert Armitage James
1889	John Owen*
1892	Watkyn Williams*

1910	John Wynne Williams
1927	John Du Buisson
1938	Vorley Spencer Ellis
1957	Harold John Charles*
1971	Charles Raymond Renowden
1993	T R Kerry Goulstone
2001	Christopher Potter
2011	Nigel Williams

*Afterwards became Bishops.

Sources

D.R. Thomas, *A History of the Diocese of St Asaph*, published by James Parker & Co, London.(1874).

Also edited by D. R. Thomas; *Y Cwtta Cyfarwydd* (a 16th Century Handbook of events in St Asaph area kept by Notary Public Peter Roberts).

Enid Bird, *The Organists and Organs of the Welsh Cathedrals in the 20th Century*, published by Enid Bird.

Archaeologia Cambrensis, 1902, 6th series, vol. 2.

John Fisher and Baring Gould, *Lives of the British Saints*.

Michael Hoy, *Isaac Barrow, His Life and Legacy*, published by Manx Heritage Foundation (2010).

John Du Buisson, *Cathedral of St Asaph*.

Raymond Renowden, *A Genial, Kind Divine: Herbert Watkyn Williams 1845 – 1944*, published by Gwasg Gee, 1998.

T. R. Kerry Goulstone, *St Asaph Cathedral: Yesterday and Today 560-1999*.

Rosemary Solbe, *The Medieval Cathedral*, (St Asaph Cathedral Guides Series No. 3).
John Hainsworth, *Sir Gilbert Scott and the Cathedral,* (St Asaph Cathedral Guides Series No. 5)
St Asaph Cathedral Website.

Acknowledgements

Alan McGuinness (interview).
Desmond Healy – First Headmaster of Ysgol Glan Clwyd, (interview).
Venerable David V. Griffith.

st davids cathedral

A Centre of Pilgrimage in a Quiet Hollow:
That's Dewi's Land,
Home of the Welsh Patron Saint.

Far away from motorways and madding crowds in the bottom left hand corner of Wales, there's St Davids, population 2000. And there in a deep hollow, the Cathedral. Here once, the field sloped steeply down to the Vallis Rosina (the Valley of the Little Swamp!) Glyn Rhosyn and the River Alun. This is the heart of Dewi's Land where he, the Patron Saint of Wales, about 1500 years ago, had his monastery, primitive structures of stone, wood, wattle and turf. This was a peaceful place to meditate in the sheltered lea of the hollow because St Davids was, as now, a windy place. Here leeks grew, and in the river's crystal clear water a ready supply of fish, enough for the mean diet of a saint. Not surprisingly he was known as the water man – Dewi Ddyfrwr. He was one of several Welsh saints, known as 'watermen' because they drank only water and as a self imposed penance, would stand up to their necks in cold water reciting the psalms. Some say he was a vegetarian too. Here he would preach to his followers and to the many who came to pay their respects – even then it was a place of pilgrimage. Nowadays it's the Mecca for 300,000 people annually. Among the Celtic Saints he was a leader, his advice sought and respected. It was from here that he went to the holy shrines of Christendom. His best known pilgrimage being to the Holy Land, Jerusalem, accompanied by fellow saints Teilo and Padarn, where the Patriarch consecrated him Archbishop. The expeditions were probably by pack-horse, fit to test the stamina of man and beast. And it was at the synod of Llanddewi Brefi c545 that he was placed 'first among the bishops of Western Britain'. David, educated at Whitland by St Paulinus, would have grown up to be Welsh speaking, but on his pilgrimages would have spoken colloquial Latin, the language he would have encountered on the way.

He was born near here at St Non's, (named after his mother Non), a site identified by the remains of a medieval church and holy well. Directly across the sea from here in Ireland, can be seen many churches dedicated to St Non and St David. In south Wales and Brittany too there are several tributes to her cult. His father was a prince of Ceredigion. Indeed in geography and temperament St Davids might easily be an Irish satellite!

So where did his knowledge of Christianity come from? The Cathedral Sub Librarian Nona Rees, a lady who has written widely about St David, says the Christian connection probably came via Glastonbury. By the 2nd century 28 priests had brought Christianity to Glastonbury and it is also claimed that Joseph of Arimathea came there with the boy Jesus even earlier. J. P. Carley states in 'Glastonbury Abbey', published by Guild Publishing in 1988, that 'David's name was found in the Calendars of Glastonbury and Sherbourne (Wessex) ...' and 'In the eighth century, Glastonbury claimed 'the blessed David' as its chief patron after Our Lady. In the tenth century, the relics of St David were claimed to be in the possession of Glastonbury, where he established a church'.

First sight of the Cathedral down Thirty Nine steps (symbolic of the 39 articles of religion) draws gasps of astonishment on account of its size and magnificence. In essence this is a Norman Church because previously in the 10th and 11th centuries Vikings using the western seaways had in their frequent raids on the Cathedral killed Bishop Morgenau (999) and Bishop Abraham (1080) and virtually destroyed the old Celtic Cathedral. By the 11th century it was a site abandoned; the Saint's shrine later discovered in undergrowth. All that remained of the pre-Norman period was a few inscribed stones including the Abraham Stone, being the gravestone of the sons of Bishop Abraham killed by the Vikings in 1080. With the coming of the Normans the achievements and independence of the Welsh Church were swept away. In 1115 Henry I appointed Bernard as the first Norman bishop of St Davids who re-organized the diocese on territorial lines. He retained St Davids as the centre of his see and lay claim to Menevia being the seat of an archbishopric: St Davids became recognised as a major centre of pilgrimage – 'once to Rome equalled twice to St Davids'. But of Bernard's Cathedral dedicated in 1131, visited by Henry II in 1171 and 1172, nothing now remains.

Rebuilding the Cathedral was begun in 1181 by Peter de Leia (Bishop 1176-98) and Giraldus de Barri, known as Gerald the Welshman, a canon of the Cathedral. Generally known as Gerald the Welshman (c1146-1223) he was christened Sylvester Giraldus de Barri and is regarded as one of the greatest Latin writers Wales has produced. Born and brought up in Manorbier Castle, Pembrokeshire of Welsh/Norman princely descent he could trace his family to one of William the Conqueror's Norman lords and to Rhys ap Tewdwr Prince of Deheubarth. He was twice thwarted in his endeavours to become Bishop of St Davids despite being eminently suited for the task on account of his undoubted intellectual and organizational abilities, his reforming zeal as well as his family connections. In the final analyses, was he perhaps too strong, far-sighted and powerful a candidate? He's now chiefly remembered for his preaching tour of Wales in 1188 in the company of Archbishop Baldwin of Canterbury recruiting support for the Third Crusade, during which he wrote vividly his impressions in the invaluable Itinierarium Cambria (1191). Several books have been written about him, his writings (his itineraries in translation) and achievements. A modern statue of Giraldus Cambrensis can be seen in a Perpendicular niche in the Cathedral's Holy Trinity Chapel, the mitre lying at his feet rather than on his head, reflecting his failure to become bishop.

The Cathedral was built in a traditional Norman style with red Cambrian sandstone from the cliffs of Caerbwdy, about one and a half miles away. The stone would have been quarried there, then brought on boats and barges along the coast to Porth Clais where the River

Alun meets the sea. They would then be manhandled the remaining short distance to the cathedral building site (stone for renovation to match the original is still available when needed from Caerbwdy). The whole building would then be lime-washed to preserve the mortar and the stone.

The Bishop's Palace built during the episcopate of Bishop Gower, 1328-48, a vast building with a copious banqueting hall, was mainly a facility for accommodating pilgrims and important visitors. The Bishop based in Abergwili Palace in Carmarthen (still the Diocesan Administrative Centre), when the pilgrims arrived, would have his horse saddled and ride to meet and greet them. Then there would be a banquet in the great hall: fish would certainly be on the menu. They would then say their prayers in the little chapels within the Palace, and in the morning they would process across to the Cathedral. In those days the Cathedral was empty: there were no pews to sit on. Proceeding to the nave, the pilgrims would go in procession around the Cathedral, chanting and waving their banners. The ruined palace is now in the care of Cadw, the Welsh concern for preserving ancient monuments, the upkeep ongoing and its value simply a testimony to a way of life long gone.

Looking carefully at the Cathedral tower from outside, an inverted V can be seen, which gives an idea of how the cathedral once appeared, a much lower building – internally darker. About 480 years ago the walls were raised and a magnificent suspended oak ceiling put in place, the carving probably done by German or Flemish craftsmen.

This then is the grandeur of a fine Cathedral, part of the great Norman legacy. Internally there is even more to admire and surprise. Dr George Middleton Vice President of The Friends of St Davids Cathedral, who first came to St Davids as a young doctor in 1954 has guided several parties around the Cathedral and is still awe-struck by its magnificence. His interest is mostly scientific but with a lively regard for the historical aspects. Dealing with the cathedral's construction before the age of bulldozers, he points out the difficulties the early builders would have encountered on a fairly steep site on suspect foundations, due to its proximity to the river. 'Levelling the area with what primitive tools they possessed would be extremely difficult' he says 'so they incorporated the slope within the building, a fall of 14 feet from one end to the other'. Finding a secure base for the footings, with an absence of rock on which to build, was yet another difficulty. This is the reason why the columns began to lean outwards. Added to that, the weight of the roof pushed the pillars out, a common fault in cathedrals, often remedied by reducing the lead in the roof.

The main side windows, of which there are ten, all vertical – a device to raise the walls and flatten the roof – are all plain glass, with one exception. In 1648, Parliamentary soldiers, intent on doing as much damage as possible including wrecking the library, destroying the organ and bells, and stripping the lead off the roof, brought their horses into the cathedral and smashed the stained glass windows. Consequently the Cathedral was roofless for two centuries. But some genius decided to collect as much as he could of the broken glass and hid them in a bucket. When, later, they got around to replacing the glass in the windows, someone remembered about the bucket and its contents, with the result that the valuable medieval glass was reassembled. 'So the window containing a double row of old stained glass around it is very important, because this is the only example of medieval coloured glass in the entire cathedral'. The other remarkable point of interest to note is that the stonework casing around the windows is all different.

The arches which are all symmetrical, each have their own distinctive pattern or carving. Dr Middleton thinks that 800 years ago they wouldn't have had architectural drawings and what happened was that they looked back at other work they had already done and said, 'Let's do it like that'. 'The nearest that they got to a plan was that the master would mould out in plaster what he wanted the craftsmen to do. So every arch has its own pattern'. Near the West door in the North West corner of the nave there's a change, quite suddenly the arch is no longer nice and round, but pointed. Moreover the pattern on the right is different from the one on the left and it's also slightly longer. The accepted explanation for this is that the whole west wall was discovered to be 3 foot out of true and this is the way they 'won' it. But they found there was no room for a tidy arch, so they had to squeeze it. 'Everywhere you go in the Cathedral you have variations in patterns' says Dr Middleton.

The rood screen between the nave and the choir was built under the direction of Bishop Henry Gower (1328-

47), who also designed and built the Bishop's Palace. All the figures on the screen are relatively modern and shows David as people thought he would have looked 1500 years ago, carrying his staff with a dove perched on his right shoulder. This pertains to one of the many tales told about David's eloquence, of how when he was out preaching at the Synod of Llanddewi Brefi someone shouted that they couldn't hear him, so he lay a handkerchief on the ground, stood on it and the land raised under him to form a small hill and a dove came and settled on his shoulder. Llanddewi Brefi village is said to stand on the spot where the miracle occurred.

Of interest, particularly to children, is the 'Mouse-man' chair by Robert Thompson the North Yorkshire craftsman who always engraved a mouse on his work. This can be seen on the right at the top end of the nave.

Of particular importance to the Cathedral is the tomb and chapel of Edmund Tudor – Earl of Richmond (d.1456) father of King Henry V11, which was originally in Grey Friars Church , Carmarthen: when St Davids became a cathedral it was moved there. When talk of the Cathedral being in Carmarthen went on in the 16th century during William Barlow's bishopric (1536-48) – on the grounds of convenience to the Bishop's Palace at Abergwili – the possibility of returning it back to Grey Friars was discussed. But the powers that be at St Davids fiercely resisted, 'so we kept the tomb and the title of the cathedral'.

The Choir is of great interest on account of the magnificent choir-stalls, one of which has a rare coat of arms: of all the cathedrals in Great Britain, St Davids is the only cathedral where the reigning monarch, is a member of the chapter, which means that this is Her Royal Highness Queen Elizabeth II's Royal Stall. Nona Rees in her admirable booklet entitled 'The Misericords of St Davids Cathedral' says, 'The choir of a medieval cathedral was like a building within a building, where worship was almost continuous. The divine offices (Matins, Lauds, Prime, Terse, Sext, None, Vespers and Compline) were said daily in addition to the Mass while standing. Aged and infirm priests were at first allowed crutches, but later as discipline eased, hinged seats were constructed in the stalls. These had a small, projecting ledge underneath, so that when the seat was raised, the occupant was supported while giving the appearance of standing. This was a deliberate concession called a misericordia (Lat. misericordia 'mercy'). These ledge seats, which from the thirteenth century onwards had a rich variety of carvings underneath them, are called misericords.' During the 500 or so intervening years the carvings, a mix of symbolism, cynicism and humour, have lost part of their significance; never the less they can in their various ways open a window on the everyday life of medieval men and women at work and play.

Looking up from here it's possible to see evidence of when the tower twice fell over, once due to bad workmanship and on the second occasion in 1248 due to an earthquake, when it fell westwards taking with it three arches. When Sir George Gilbert Scott surveyed the building in 1862 he reported his concern for its parlous condition, particularly the tower, which was in imminent danger of collapse. Remarkably he succeeded in rebuilding the tower without taking it down. Two large plates tightly bolted at the outside, using, according to local legend, heat from lighted candles to aid their screwing up, ensures that after 150 years the tower remains upstanding!

David's presence is deeply felt within the Cathedral, but the question remains unanswered as to where lie his mortal remains. For years it was believed that they were in a casket located in the Cathedral walls: bones thus buried were always considered to be those of very important people. The casket contained the bones of two people, one tall thought to be those of St David and of a shorter person reputed to be those of St Justinian, (St David's friend and collaborator). But carbon dating a fragment of these remains has shown that the bones are about 400 years short of St Davids time and therefore the Saint's remains must be elsewhere!

Central to St David's importance as a destination for the faithful is his shrine. In the 12th century Pope Calixtus II declared St Davids to be a place of pilgrimage and it was at this time that the medieval shrine was constructed and placed close to the High Altar. The Pope emphasised its importance: this was to be a point of focus for pilgrims, two pilgrimages to St Davids were the equivalent of one to Rome, three were equivalent to one to Jerusalem. Damaged during the Reformation, later by Cromwell's cavalry and showing signs of wear, St David's Shrine is now badly in need of restoration: the challenge to raise £150,000 required to do this has been taken on by the 'Friends of St David's Cathedral'.

The Bishop of St Davids looks after the entire Diocese of St Davids, from Aberystwyth in the north down most of the way to Swansea, a huge area which was even larger before 1923 when the new Diocese of Swansea and Brecon was created. The administration is done from Abergwili, but the Cathedral is the responsibility of the Dean who lives in the Deanery which is some 200 yards away from the Cathedral. The Chapter duties are best described as caring for the Cathedral fabric and worship. Each member of which have their own stall and for a special service come to the seat to which they're appointed.

The Friends of the Cathedral raise a lot of money for cathedral needs, for example raising funds for the restoration of the St David Shrine and currently 'we have three choral scholars sponsored during their 'gap' year'. Having done their A. Levels in music, some will sing others will play the organ.

Cathedral Library: Book Browsers Paradise!

The Cathedral Sub-Librarian Nona Rees is a native of Carmarthen, where her father Canon Thomas Haliwell was principal of Trinity College. Her father was very friendly with Dean Parry then dean of St Davids: thus began the St Davids connection and a decision to buy a house there where he spent his retirement. 'We all adored St Davids' she says. That's where she gravitated to after a career which basically began at Aberystwyth University, where she took a degree in English and a teachers training course. 'But I soon discovered that teaching was the last thing I wanted to do' she says. So she decided to do a one year Graduate Secretarial Course in Cardiff. She had evidently found her niche and a secretarial career followed: firstly to the Statistics Professor at Aberystwyth then later, by then married, Secretary to the Professor of Oceanography at Bangor in North Wales. When the children came along she eventually trailed back to St Davids and has 'been here ever since'. As the children were growing up she got a post as Community Librarian in St Davids. And following her retirement took up the position in 1997 of St Davids Cathedral Sub-Librarian.

Immersed in an institution which goes back to Medieval times, but was moved to the Chapter Room, where it now is since the 19th century, Nona Rees has a handsome collection of ancient books and documents (the earliest dating back to 1505) in her care. In essence it's a library in two parts, one based on books given by Dean Alan and built on since, and the second, the library from Abergwili Palace. For a modest lending fee readers can make their selection. Or browse a 1717 Browne Willis edition of his survey of St Davids; original John Speed (1610) maps, Arch Cam editions to the present day and a photographic collection of old photos of the area.

With all this at her elbow there is little wonder that Nona Rees, herself an author of several books on St David including 'Medieval Shrines of St Davids Cathedral', 'St David of Dewisland' and 'Pilgrimage on a Welsh Perspective', is often the first port of call for Dewi information. 'Some I can answer quite quickly' she says, 'others may take a little longer!'

More about the Library

Origins go back to Medieval times when clerics transcribed and illuminated manuscripts here. Richly illustrated mss of Gospels, Psalters and other texts were destroyed during the Reformation and any work Catholic in nature suffered the same fate. More destruction followed in 1648 when parliamentary soldiers descended on St David Cathedral and burnt anything considered to be sacrilegious. Despite this sordid history, St Davids Cathedral Library has over 7000 books in its collection.

St Davids has a tradition of scholarship that can be traced back to its very beginnings. When King Alfred needed help to rebuild the intellectual life of Wessex after being decimated by the Vikings he called on Asser the bishop of St Davids to help him. This reputation for scholarship continues today embodied in the Cathedral Library.

The origins of the library lie in the monastery of St David which stood here before the cathedral was built, a scriptorium where monks wrote and illustrated manuscripts and documents. Despite much of the collection being destroyed during the turbulent years of the 16th and 17th centuries the Library contains some truly remarkable treasures.

Music at the Cathedral

The first reference to an organ at St Davids Cathedral was in 1490 when Walter Warryn was paid forty shillings for playing one. And there's a further reference in 1565: 'for making two stops for ye great Organs' at a cost of 6d. Later, in 1581, an order was made by the Bishop for a new organ to be made 'ad usum divini servitii'. All that is known about this instrument is that it was placed under the western arch of the tower on the rood screen. July 26th 1698 sees a decision by the Chantor and Chapter 'to provide an organ with all convenient speed': the work to be entrusted to the celebrated Bernard Schmidt (better known as 'Father Smith') at a cost of £290. This organ stood on the rood screen, its casework made of Norwegian oak supposedly carved by Grinling Gibbons. It had one manual and no pedals. In 1843 the organ was rebuilt, re-sited and enlarged by Lincoln.

The organ was not in use from 1865 to 1883, the period when George Gilbert Scott was working on the Cathedral. At the end of this time a decision was taken to have a new organ built and 'Father' Henry Willis was contracted to do the work.

In 1900 Vincent Willis added the Pedal Trombone. The organ was rebuilt in 1906 and further alterations made in 1920-21. On September 7th 1945 Cathedral Organist Joseph Soar requested that the Dean should contact Messrs Willis and Sons regarding the condition of the organ blower. The required wind pressure at this time was produced using water power, there being no electricity at the Cathedral. Since the organ in the Tabernacle Chapel was powered by the same water supply as the Cathedral, stories were told that when when the Cathedral Organ was being played the chapel organ was short of wind!

The Henry Willis Organ of 1883 underwent a rebuild by Hill Norman and Beard in 1953: no significant tonal alterations were made, save that the instrument was housed in a new case by the architect Alban Caroe. Being smaller than the previous 'pipe-rack' by Willis meant that almost the entire pedal organ had to be moved off the screen to a new enclosure in the South Transept. This created enormous problems of balance: these pipes were too loud in the quire but not loud enough in the Nave. Further work took place in 1980 by Rushworth and Dreaper, and Percy Daniel and Co in 1986 and1989.

The organ was dismantled in September 1998 and underwent a major restoration and rebuild by Harrison & Harrison of Durham between 1998 and 2000. A new case of limed oak (incorporating parts of the old east case) once again houses almost the entire pedal organ on screen, the Willis Choir removed in 1980 was re-instated, and with a few other additions in the style of Father Willis, the new organ now has four manuals and fifty-four stops.

The new instrument was dedicated by the Bishop of St Davids at Choral Matins on Sunday October 15th 2000 and the inaugural recital given by Dr Roy Massey MBE, then organist of Hereford Cathedral on Wednesday 15th of November 2000.

The Organist and Master of the Choristers, and Director of the St Davids Music Festival since September 2007 is Alexander Mason.

Mr Mason was born in Cheltenham in 1974 where he became a chorister, and from the age of fifteen, Organ Scholar at Gloucester Cathedral under Dr John Saunders. He then went on to study at Worcester College (Organ Scholar); The Royal Conservatory, The Hague (Improvisation) and The Royal College of Music (Choral Conducting). His teachers were David Sanger, Jos van der Kooy and Paul Spicer. He became an FRCO aged eighteen winning the Turpin, Durant and Dixon prizes and later received awards from the Countess of Munster, Ian Fleming and Eric Thompson Trusts.

He moved to London in 1995 and was subsequently Organ Scholar at St Brides Church, Fleet Street, Assistant Organist at HM Chapel Royal, Hampton Court Palace and Director of Music at All Saints, Fulham. During this time he was also Organist of King's College, Wimbledon, and music assistant for English National Opera's 'The Knack', acting Sub-Organist at Guildford and Southwark Cathedrals and the conductor of a number of choirs.

He was Assistant Organist at Lichfield Cathedral from 2002 to 2007 where he was also founder-Director of Lichfield Cathedral School Girls' Choir, Associate Conductor of the Cathedral's Chamber Choir and directed Music Share, Lichfield Cathedral's programme of musical outreach. Also a tutor in improvisation at Birmingham Conservatoire.

Since his arrival at St Davids he has directed the Cathedral Choir in broadcasts on BBC Radio 3 & 4 and S4C, two CDs for Regent Records, and a successful tour of Bulgaria. He has directed the choir in first performances of commissions by David Briggs, Mark Blatchly and Alexander L'Estrange. And recorded two further CDs with the Boys' Choir and as a solo organist. In addition he's overseen the establishment of choral scholarships and a programme of musical outreach to local schools. All this in addition to preparing the cathedral choirs for the Sunday services!

'When I came here in 2007 there were only two boys in the choir' says Alexander Mason, 'I've built them up so that at the end of 2009 we had twenty-one and they come from as far south as Tenby and as far north as St Dogmaels. I get around the schools recruiting; being a sparsely populated area it's not easy – that's why the boys choir has fluctuated astonishingly over the last twenty years. But there are a lot of children out there and there isn't an awful lot else for them to do'.

He will listen to as many children as want to sing, sometimes listening to an entire year group.

'One year I heard two hundred children, but from that number it's only a few who'll want to join'. No stone is left unturned, sometimes he'll make a spectacular discovery – a child whose talent has not been picked on. 'People don't realise what we do and the opportunities we have here. The best way is to go out and make face to face contact and tell the children what we can offer them' he says.

'The music organization within Pembrokeshire seems

to be more instrumentally based. The Cathedral is the only place, it seems to me, providing opportunities for young choral singers'.

The child choristers are drawn from secondary schools at St Davids, Fishguard and Haverfordwest and local primary ones at Roach, Solva and others in the vicinity. Their ages range from eight to eighteen: most of the girls come from the secondary schools – attending rehearsals at 4.30, after school hours. He also runs a junior choir which meet for singing practice at 3.45 on Fridays, currently it's eighteen strong – but has been as high as thirty-five. Many will later progress to their respective Cathedral Choir. During their time as choir members they will be taught the basics of music including sight reading off the score. In all this he will have his assistant organist, Simon Pearce whose been here since 1998, playing the organ for the services when the choir is involved and assisting with training the probationers. Simon a native of Wakefield in West Yorkshire was born in 1974 and is a former Head Chorister at Wakefield Cathedral. After graduating with honours from the University of Hull, where he was awarded the Sir Thomas Beecham Scholarship, he moved to Rippon Cathedral as an organ scholar and studied with Kerry Beaumont. Upon his appointment to St Davids he also became Assistant Conductor of the Cathedral Festival Choir and assumed responsibility for the Cathedral's voluntary adult Choir now known as the 'Cathedral Singers'.

So St Davids has three choirs: a junior choir, a boys choir, and a girls choir which also includes the Lay

Clerks (comprising of clergy – the Dean is a tenor – and others, all local people). Additionally there's a small group known as the Cathedral Singers of which Nona Rees is an alto member, their Choirmaster being Assistant Organist Simon Pearce. This is an auditioned choir with very exacting standards and sing evensong once a fortnight.

Early during Alexander Mason's tenure the custom of having three choral scholars was introduced. They will stay here during their gap year singing with the boys choir and honing their musical abilities.

'The future of music is assured here', says Mr Mason 'with constant hard work we're always looking to the next generation, at the moment its in a strong base'. But he accepts that choir membership requires tremendous commitment. 'In addition the children have to sing on Christmas Day and at the St Davids Musical Festival which is held during their Summer Half-term holidays. So we do ask an awful lot, but they love it and get good rewards. Parents can see they get one of the few opportunities in Pembrokeshire for excellence. It's very important for the children to have this sense of commitment and high standards: it rubs off on everything else that they do and they get an awareness of community'.

Briefly

c589 (?602)	Death of St David, March 1.
645-1097	Menevia ravaged, burnt or destroyed on 13 occasions.
999	Vikings kill Bishop Morgenau.
1080	Vikings kill Bishop Abraham.
1081	William the Conqueror visits.
1089	David's Shrine vandalized.
1115	Bernard becomes bishop.
1131	Dedication of church.
1171 and 1172	Henry II visits.
1181-82	Present cathedral begun by Bishop Peter de Leia and Giraldus Cambrensis, Gerald the Welshman.
1220	The new tower collapses.
c1247	Building affected by earthquake.
1275	The shrine of St David built.
1328-47	Gower's episcopate: rood screen and Bishops' Palace built.
1365	St Mary's College built.
1509-22	Edward Vaughan's episcopate: Holy Trinity Chapel built.
1530-40	Nave roof and ceiling built.
1538	Destruction of shrine.
1540	Edmund Tudor's tomb brought to St Davids.
1648	Destruction of building by Parliamentary soldiers.
1793	Nash rebuilds the west front.
1862-77	Gilbert Scott's restorations.

1900-10	Eastern chapels restored.
1982	Queen Elizabeth II distributes the Royal Maundy.
1993	St David's Day celebrations with the Prince of Wales.
1995	City status conferred.
1998-2001	West front refaced, organ rebuilt; Porth y Twr re-roofed.

The Bishop

The Bishop of St Davids Cathedral since September 2008 is the Very Revd John Wyn Evans who was previously Dean of the Cathedral for fourteen years. A native of Llandeloy about seven miles from St Davids, he grew up at Aberystwyth, where his father the Rev. Eifion Evans was Vicar, and was educated at the local Ardwyn Grammar School before going on to the University of Wales Cardiff where he studied archaeology. He trained for the Ministry at St Michael's College, Llandaff from 1968 to 1971.

John Wyn Evans, popularly known as Wyn, served his early priesthood as a minor canon at St Davids from 1972 to 1975. After a couple of years researching at Oxford University he returned to Pembrokeshire where he served as Rector of Llanfallteg with Clunderwen and Henllan Amgoed with Llangan from 1977 to 1982. He was Diocesan Warden of Ordinants from 1975 to 1983, Chaplain of Trinity College of Carmarthen 1982 to 1990 and Diocesan Director of Education 1983 to1992; made an honorary Canon at St Davids Cathedral in 1988 and a Canon from 1990 to 1994. From 1990 to 1994 a Dean of Chapel at Trinity College Carmarthen and Head of the Department of Religious Studies. He was made Dean and Presenter of St Davids Cathedral in 1994. From 1994 to 2001, he was Vicar of St Davids, a parish which was enlarged into a Rectorial Benefice and renamed Dewisland in 2001, where he served as Rector.

Bishop Wyn who is a keen historian, an acknowledged authority on the lives of the early Welsh saints and St Davids Cathedral, has edited a recently published book, 'St David of Wales – Cult, Church and Nation'. And is an honorary fellow of the University of Wales Lampeter. He is married to Diane who is a professional potter in St Davids.

The Dean

The Dean of St Davids since 2008 is The Very Revd Jonathan Lean who is a native of nearby Fishguard (b. 1952). He felt the call to the ministry at an early age and became actively involved, as a youth, in both the parishes of Fishguard and Goodwick. He began his training for the priesthood in 1971 at Burgess Hall Lampeter. And after completion in 1974 went on to the College of the Resurrection, Mirfield for a further year's study before his ordination as a deacon in July 1975 and priesting in the following year. He then served a six year curacy at Tenby before in 1981 becoming vicar of Llanrhian, Llanhywel and Llanrheithlan. In 1988 he accepted an invitation to be Vicar of St Martin's Haverfordwest and of St Ishmael's Lambstone. In 2000 appointed Canon Residentiary of St David's Cathedral and in 2001 Team Vicar of the newly created Rectorial Benefice of Dewisland with responsibility for St Davids parish.

The Dean is keenly interested in music, involved with local choirs for many years, he sings tenor in the Cathedral Choir and with the John S, Davies Singers; and he's also Chairman of the St Davids Cathedral Festival.

St Davids Cathedral

Bishop of St Davids: The Very Revd John Wyn Evans.
Dean of St Davids: The Very Revd Jonathan Lean.
Director of Music: Mr Daniel Cook (formerly Assistant Director of Music at Salisbury Cathedral, took up the post in November 2011 in succession to Alexander Mason).
Cathedral Office: The Deanery Office, St Davids Cathedral, The Close, St Davids, Pembrokeshire. SA62 6RH. Tel. 01437 720 202
e-mail: info@stdavidscathedral.org.uk
Website: www.stdavidscathedral.org.uk

Times of Services

Sundays:
8.00am	Holy Communion
9.30am	Cymun Bendigaid (Capel Mair)

9.30am	Parish Eucharist (Nave)
11.15am	Choral Matins
6.00pm	Choral Evensong

4th Sunday of every month:

7.30am	Morning Prayer
8.00am	Holy Communion(1662)
9.30am	Cymun Bendigaid (Capel Mair)
9.30am	Family Eucharist (Nave)
11.15am	Choral Eucharist
6.00pm	Choral Evensong

Daily Services (apart from Wednesday):

| 8.00am | Morning Prayer and Holy Communion |
| 6.00pm | Evening Prayer or Choral Evensong |

Wednesday:

8.00am	Boreuol Weddi a Cymun Bendigaid
10.00am	Holy Communion
6.00pm	Evening Prayer

Bishops

(1023)	Morgeneu
1023	Ervin
1039	Trahaearn
(1061)	Joseph
1061	Bleiddud
1071	Sulien
1076	Abraham

1078	Sulien (again)
1085	Wilfrid
1115	Bernard
1147	David Fitz-Gerald
1176	Peter de Leiâ
1204	Geoffrey de Henelawe
1215	Iorwerth alias Gervase
1230	Anselm le Gras
1284 ??	Thomas Wallensis
1256	Richard de Carew
1280	Thomas Beck
1293	David Martyn
1328	Henry de Gower
1347	John Thoresby
1350	Reginald Brian
1353	Thomas Fastolfe
1361	Adam Houghton
1389	John Gilbert
1397	Guy Mone
1408	Henry Chichely
1414	John Catterick
1415	Stephen Patrington
1418	Benedict Nicholls
1433	Thomas Rodburne
1442	William Lyndwood
1447	John Langton
1447	John Delabere
1460	Robert Tully
1482	Richard Martin
1483	Thomas Langton
1485	Hugh Pavy

1496	John Morgan
1505	Robert Sherborne
1509	Edward Vaughan
1523	Richard Rawlins
1536	William Barlow
1548	Robert Ferrar
1554	Henry Morgan
1559	Thomas Young
1561	Richard Davies
1582	Marmaduke Middleton
1594	Anthony Rudd
1615	Richard Milbourne
1621	William Laud
1627	Theophilus Field
1635	Roger Mainwaring
1660	William Lucy
1677	William Thomas
1683	Laurence Womack
1686	John Lloyd
1687	Thomas Watson
1705	George Bull
1710	Philip Bisse
1713	Adam Ottley
1723	Richard Smallbrooke
1730	Elias Sydall
1731	Nicholas Claggett
1742	Edward Willes
1743	Hon Richard Trevor
1752	Anthony Ellis
1761	Samuel Squire
1766	Robert Lowth

1766	Charles Moss
1774	Hon James Yorke
1779	John Warren
1783	Edward Smallwell
1788	Samuel Horsley
1793	Hon William Stuart
1800	Lord George Murray
1803	Thomas Burgess
1825	John Banks Jenkinson
1840	Connop Thirlwall
1874	Basil Jones
1897	John Owen
1927	D. L. Prosser
1950	W. T. Havard
1957	John R. Richards
1971	Eric M. Roberts
1982	George Noakes
1991	J. Ivor Rees
1996	Huw Jones
2002	Carl N. Cooper
2009	J. Wyn Evans

Deans

1839	Llewelyn Llewellin (assumed title of Dean in 1840)
1878	James Allen
1897	Evan Owen Phillips
1897	David Howell
1904	James Allan Smith

1919	William Williams
1931	David Watcyn Morgan
1940	Albert W. Parry
1950	Carlyle Witton-Davies
1957	T. Edward Jenkins
1972	Lawrence Bowen
1984	A. Gordon MacWilliam
1990	Bertie Lewis
1994	J. Wyn Evans
2009	D. Jonathan R. Lean

Organists

1490	Priest Vicars
1509	John Norman
1563	Thomas Elliot
1577	Priest Vicars
1713	R. Mordant
1714	Henry Mordant
1719	Richard Tomkins
1719	Williarn Bishop
1720	Henry Williams
1725	Matthew Maddox
1734	Matthew Philpott
1793	Arthur Richardson
1827	John Barrett
1851	William Peregrine Propert
1883	Frederick Garton
1894	D. John Codner
1896	Herbert C. Morris

1922	Joseph Soar
1953	Peter Boorman
1977	Nicholas Jackson
1984	Malcolm Watts
1990	Kerry Beaumont
1995	Geraint Bowen
2001	Timothy Noon
2007	Alexander Mason
2011	Daniel Cook

Sources

St Davids Cathedral, (The Pitkin Guide) Authorised by the Dean and Chapter.

Friends of St Davids Cathedral Annual Report 2009 and 2010.

St Davids and North Pembrokeshire, by D. G. Hampson (1974 edition).

The Cathedrals, Abbeys & Priories of Wales, by Tim McCormick, published Logaston Press 2010.

St David of Dewisland, by Nona Rees, published Gomer Press 1992.

The Misericords of St Davids Cathedral Pembrokeshire, by Nona Rees, published RJL Smith & Associates, Much Wenlock, Shropshire (for St Davids Cathedral).

The Organists and Organs of the Welsh Cathedrals in the 20th Century, compiled by Enid Bird, published by Enid Bird, 16 Miller Ave, Wakefield, West Yorkshire. WF2 7DJ.

Gerald of Wales, by Robert M. Morris, published

University of Wales Press 1997.

St Davids Cathedral website.

St David of Wales, Cult, Church and Nation, edited by J. Wyn Evans and Jonathan M. Wooding, published in 2007 by The Boydell Press, Woodbridge.

Dr George Middleton, Vice President of 'Friends of St David's Cathedral' (Interview).

Nona Rees, Sub Librarian of St Davids Cathedral (Interview).

Alexander Mason, Cathedral Organist and Musical Director. (Interview).

appendix

List of Archbishops:

1920-1934	Alfred Edwards
1934-1944	Charles Green
1944-1949	David Prosser
1949-1957	John Morgan
1957-1967	Edwin Morris
1968-1971	Glyn Simon
1971-1982	Gwilym Williams
1983-1986	Derrick Childs
1987-1991	George Noakes
1991-1999	Alwyn Rice Jones
1999-2002	Rowan Williams
2002-	Barry Morgan

On-line Shop

Our whole catalogue of titles are
available on our website

• Walking and Mountaineering
• Regions of Wales/Local Guides
• Maritime Wales
•Welsh Heritage and Culture
• Art and Photography
• Welsh History and Myths
• Children's Books
❊ BARGAINS ❊

www.carreg-gwalch.com

Further enjoyable reading on History and Heritage

Visit our website for further information:
www.carreg-gwalch.com

Orders can be placed on our
On-line Shop

Heritage

Visit our website for further information:
www.carreg-gwalch.com

Orders can be placed on our
On-line Shop

Photography and Text

Visit our website for further information:
www.carreg-gwalch.com

Orders can be placed on our
On-line Shop